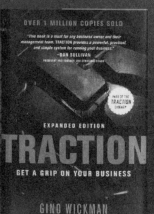

THE TRACTION LIBRARY

GETTING EVERYONE IN YOUR COMPANY ON THE SAME PAGE

TRACTION: GET A GRIP ON YOUR BUSINESS
Strengthen the Six Key Components™ of your business using simple yet powerful tools and disciplines.

FOR EVERYONE

GET STARTED:

ROCKET FUEL: THE ONE ESSENTIAL COMBINATION
Dive into how the Visionary and Integrator™ duo can take their company to new heights.

FOR VISIONARIES & INTEGRATORS

GET A GRIP: AN ENTREPRENEURIAL FABLE
Follow this fable's characters as they learn how to run on EOS® and address real-world business situations.

FOR THE LEADERSHIP TEAM

WHAT THE HECK IS EOS?
Create ownership and buy-in from every employee in your organization, inspiring them to take an active role in achieving your company's vision.

FOR ALL EMPLOYEES, MANAGERS, & SUPERVISORS

HOW TO BE A GREAT BOSS!
Help bosses at all levels of your organization get the most from their people.

FOR LEADERS, MANAGERS, & SUPERVISORS

THE EOS LIFE
Learn how to create your ideal life by doing what you love, with people you love, making a huge difference, being compensated appropriately, and with time for other passions.

FOR ENTREPRENEURS & LEADERSHIP TEAMS

THE EOS MASTERY SERIES
Dive deeper into each of the Six Key Components for more masterful execution.

EOSWORLDWIDE.COM/TRACTION-LIBRARY

PRAISE FOR *PEOPLE*

"*People: Dare to Build an Intentional Culture* brilliantly captures the transformative power of intentional company culture. As a great addition to the Traction Library, it underscores that at the core of every successful business are its people. A vital read for any leader aiming for more than just business as usual."

—Gino Wickman, author of *Traction* and *Shine* and creator of EOS

"*People* is the most consequential book you'll read all year. The authors emphasize the undeniable: get the people aspect right or risk everything. EOS, with its signature clarity, dives deep into the core issues and offers entrepreneurs a blueprint to transform ideas into results. Where many leaders see a challenge, this book reveals a competitive advantage. You need *People*!"

**—David Kolbe, Visionary and CEO of Kolbe Corp
and expert on human performance**

"I love this book! As someone who's passionate about entrepreneurial teamwork, I'm so impressed—*People* is an incredible how-to manual for how to attract, develop, and retain great team members by having an intentional culture. As I read it, I kept thinking of everyone I wanted to read it—it's that good. A must-read for anyone who cares about both people and profits."

—Shannon Waller, entrepreneurial team strategist, strategic coach, and author of *The Team Success Handbook* and *Multiplication by Subtraction*

"The subtitle of this book tells it all! Daring takes courage; the Latin word, *cor*, meaning heart, is the root of the word courage. In order to build an intentional culture, therefore, a leader must drop into their heart, and have the courage to move from fear to love. Not only does this book come from the heart, the authors have done a fantastic job tying the importance of intentionality, courage, and commitment to a strong people component in your business. *People* offers another valuable building block to help entrepreneurs find freedom toward living their ideal lives."

—Alex Freytag, expert EOS Implementer, author of *Profit Works*, and creator of ProfitWorks

"Our people, and our level of intentionality in nourishing and cultivating culture, can make or break the success and impact of a business. *People* is an essential puzzle piece of the EOS tools and methodology to building an intentional and powerful culture."

—Anese Cavanaugh, CEO of Active Choices, Inc., creator of IEP Method®, founder of Positive Energy Workplace Initiative, and author of *Contagious Culture, Contagious You* and *The Leader You Will Be*

"With over 15,000 companies running on EOS, the authors have revealed what they've discovered. That it takes effort and intention to build the right culture for the right people in the right seats. Filled with practical applications and stories of intentionally building a culture where humans thrive, this book is the catalyst and guidebook that will help you and your leadership team get on the same page with the culture YOU intend to build!"

—Jill Young, expert EOS Implementer, head coach at EOS Worldwide, and author of The Advantage Series

"*People* is my new handbook for the most fundamental part of the business—our people. As an Integrator, I'm already using this book as a key resource for myself and my team. It seamlessly blends practical advice and real-world examples while giving you everything you need to handle your most important people opportunities. A must-have for every leader!"

—Amy Bruske, Integrator and president of Kolbe Corp and expert on human performance

"The message of *People* resonates very well with my 'people-first' mindset when creating a healthy and productive environment in which to effectively lead employees. It hits on all the vital areas that are needed to develop an engaging workplace in any industry. But the key word here is 'intentional' and that's why this book is a must-read for any entrepreneur or team leader who sincerely wants to lay down a strong foundation on which to build and grow a successful business and transform the people around them."

—Sunny Kaila, founder and CEO of IT By Design
and author of *Talentpreneurship*

"The people are the work. Without people, nothing happens. Kelly, CJ, and Mark have laid the groundwork for unlocking sustainable growth within the EOS framework. When you lead and manage well, you begin the journey of intentionally managing human energy with heart. You'll be inspired and challenged as you focus on what most entrepreneurs struggle to make the time for—elevating your team. This book offers a path for doing the work to produce leaders who produce leaders. If you're tired of being surrounded by helpers and are ready to catalyze your team to be their best, read this book, answer the questions within it and do the work. Your team will thank you for it."

—Sue Hawkes, expert EOS Implementer, CEO of
YESS!, and author of *Chasing Perfection*

"I have always stayed away from the word *culture*; I thought of it as a poorly defined, namby-pamby, academic word that is often tossed about and used by people with an idea but no real-world sets and reps to back up how they were using the word. Until today, when I finished reading *People*. Since 2008, I have heard Gino describe EOS as a 'human energy system.' We reveal that EOS is a 'trust building program' at each Two-Day Annual™ and we describe EOS as delivering Vision Traction Healthy™ (VTH). These words get close but do not quite hit the nail squarely on the head. But now CJ, Kelly, and Mark have boiled down what we do as

EOS Implementers™ into two words. We help owners and leaders create and maintain their own unique intentional culture, the culture that must exist in order for them to enjoy their EOS Life™. Sets and reps: our coauthors and EOS are not practicing on you. Since 2007, EOS Implementers have helped over 25,621 companies (our sets) across more than 250,334 eight-hour session days (our reps) install the simple tools and disciplines required to create and maintain intentional culture. In addition to pulling on this huge body of work, our authors CJ and Mark have over 2,107 session days (reps) and have directly helped over 249 companies (sets) create their intentional culture. Kelly, as Integrator of EOS Worldwide working with Mark, our Visionary, drives the intentional culture of the mothership using EOS—they practice what they preach. This morning, I love the word *culture*, as long as it is combined with the word intentional. Intentional culture, intentional culture, intentional culture—that just feels right. Thank you, CJ, Kelly, and Mark."

—Walt Brown, expert EOS Implementer since 2008, author of *The Patient Organization*, *Death of the Org Chart*, *Rise of the Organizational Graph*, and *Attract or Repel*

PEOPLE

PEOPLE

DARE TO BUILD AN INTENTIONAL CULTURE

MARK O'DONNELL, KELLY KNIGHT, CJ DUBE'

WITH DAVID MOFFITT

BenBella Books, Inc.
Dallas, TX

BenBella Books, Inc.
10440 N. Central Expressway
Suite 800
Dallas, TX 75231
benbellabooks.com
Send feedback to feedback@benbellabooks.com
BenBella is a federally registered trademark.

Printed in the United States of America
10 9 8 7 6 5 4 3 2 1

Library of Congress Control Number: 2023044520
ISBN 9781637744369 (print)
ISBN 9781637744376 (ebook)

Copyediting by Ginny Glass
Proofreading by Denise Pangia and Cape Cod Compositors, Inc.
Text design and composition by Aaron Edmiston
Cover design by Sarah Avinger
Printed by Lake Book Manufacturing

Special discounts for bulk sales are available.
Please contact bulkorders@benbellabooks.com.

For Rachel, Ava, Quinn, and Nora—my rock, my heart.

*And for every Leader, Manager, and EOS Implementer who
helps people find their best lives. This book is for you.*
—Mark O'Donnell

*To my parents, Pat and Kathy Jones, who taught me from my
earliest memories that love and kindness endure above all things
and who gave me the confidence to learn, grow, and fly.*

*And also to my husband, Tim, my son, Ryan, and my daughters
Katie and Lauren, I love you with all my heart and soul.*

*Finally, for all who dream of making a huge impact in the
world and serving others well, this book is for you.*
—Kelly Knight

*To my wonderful large family who keep me energized and motivated
to constantly work on mastery. With love Bob DuBe' my husband
who keeps me grounded. My children Alex, Nicki, RJ, Samantha,
Erin, Taylor, and Logan and all their beautiful better halves. My
grandchildren who keep me young—Maddie, Max, Braydon, Rylan,
Mackenzie, Grace, Owen, Olivia, Skylar, Natalie, Lydia, and Knox.*

*For our amazing Community of Implementers, Leaders, Managers,
and Owners who change lives every day. This book is for you to
continue breaking through ceilings to live your best lives!*
—CJ DuBe'

CONTENTS

FOREWORD

Have you ever really considered what an honor it is to lead people in your company? Have you reflected on the impact you can have on their well-being, purposefulness, and the quality of their work lives? What a magnificent gift, one that's both an opportunity and a responsibility.

Many business leaders feel the burden of the responsibility without knowing how to make the most of the opportunity. I see this every day in working with the clients of my company, Active Choices.

These leaders struggle to understand what it means to truly transform a culture. They often think, at first, they're looking for a fast checklist, a quick culture transformer, or a one-hour workshop that will forever solve their "people problems."

One of the key themes you'll find in these pages is that surface-level solutions and quick fixes never take hold. This completely aligns with my own experiences working with leaders. Only true courage and deep commitment can create an amazing culture.

But once you have the commitment, how is it done? What are the keys to building an intentional culture? This book will give you the answers to those questions. And one of the most important answers is this: how you show up as a leader on a consistent basis is crucial to success or failure in culture building.

This is where the concept of what I call your Intentional Energetic Presence®, or your IEP, can be helpful. IEP is all about how you show up as a leader, and the intentions, energy, and presence you bring to everything you do.

The IEP you personally bring to this process will be a vital ingredient of a great culture. You can see this as another process you *do* (checklists, tools, or initiatives), or you can see it as a way of being and thinking that you *become* (that you learn to embody). Committing to becoming and embodying what you want your culture to be is the path to transformation.

Don't misunderstand me. In leadership, we need both the doing and the being. After twenty-plus years helping to create authentic positive-energy workplaces, I have found many times over that tools, trainings, and frameworks are often necessary, brilliant, and helpful. But not enough by themselves.

If the IEPs of the leader and team aren't clean and clear and grounded, all the greatest tools and frameworks in the world will only go so far and, in some cases, may possibly do more harm than good.

For example, have you ever been given (possibly very important) feedback, but the way the person delivered it was so laden with judgment that you couldn't hear the value behind it? Or been given feedback by a person who was simply not present or caring, and that made it impossible to receive it, no matter how accurate? The feedback giver's IEP is blocking the gift that should have been delivered with intention, helpful energy, and presence.

Have you ever attended a training that introduced you to several great new tools, but the energy of the training was so *blah* that the tools failed to stick? That's a lack of IEP working against excellent training and lessening its impact.

You can see this in meetings too. You may notice a team member who consistently seems to suck the life out of the room (they're the "lowest vibration in the room," as we say in the IEP methodology). Their energy, lack of presence, facial expressions, posture, and comments (or lack of comments) make the meeting feel like something everyone has to trudge through.

Others in the room feel this and then either match it, lowering their own vibrations (because IEP is contagious) or spend their time and energy trying to manage or work around it.

Sometimes it's your own IEP that may be a problem. Have you ever had a time when you did all the right things to prepare for a conversation as a leader, but then when you had that conversation, it didn't land with the impact you wanted? Perhaps you were frustrated or distracted or exhausted or simply not fully present.

Most often, missed impact is directly related to our IEP.

All of this may sound a little foreign at first, maybe even a bit too intangible. That's understandable. We often spend days with leaders, getting them to understand the nuance of their IEP, how it impacts their leadership and culture, what to do about it, and how to authentically optimize it.

Here is how to understand it better. Read through this book carefully and attentively (with intention). Commit and start implementing what you learn. As you do this, make a conscious effort to bring your best intention, energy, and presence to building a great culture. All of this fits together, and your understanding grows as you begin to see and feel the impact in your business.

And make no mistake: it will make an impact. The concepts, tools, and frameworks that you need to build an intentional culture are between these covers; the better your intentions, energy, and presence as a leader, the more positive impact you'll have.

I've been a fan of EOS for years. Their models and tools have been integrated into Active Choices since 2018 in various ways. I've been grateful from the start to have the clarity that the Accountability Chart, the People Analyzer, the V/TO, and so many other tools and methods bring to our team.

So when Mark, Kelly, and CJ told me they were writing a book to dig deep into the People Component, I was excited. Then when they asked me to do the foreword, I was thrilled. Because I know that all three of them understand that people matter more than anything else to your business. Without our people, we have nothing. Period.

The way forward is to optimize culture, and for that, you need intention, love, tools, and solid action. Mark, Kelly, CJ, and many others are sharing incredibly powerful resources, frameworks, and real-life stories of EOS tools in action to guide your organization's transformation.

May this book serve as a road map on your own authentic journey as a leader. Apply the tools and principles, take care of yourself as a leader, bring your own love and intention to the table, and move forward with your team to become a high-impact, positively contagious culture.

With great intention, gratitude, and so much love for you and your business,

Anese

Anese Cavanaugh
CEO, Active Choices, Inc. | Creator, IEP Method®
Founder, Positive Energy Workplace Initiative™
Author, *Contagious Culture, Contagious You,*
and *The Leader You Will Be*
Anese@ActiveChoices.com

. . . .

CHAPTER 1

CHAOS OR INTENTIONAL CULTURE?

"YOUR LIFE DOESN'T GET BETTER BY CHANCE,
IT GETS BETTER BY CHANGE"
—JIM ROHN

We always survey the businesses that choose to work with an Entrepreneurial Operating System (EOS) and ask them what motivated them to do it. Eighty-two percent of them say this:

"I was not getting enough out of my people. We weren't all on the same page, working together to win."

This is by far the most common answer as to why they decided to make changes to their business. In fact, it was more than *double* any other reason given.

EOS has worked with tens of thousands of companies, and hundreds of thousands of individuals, and we're not at all surprised by the number of business owners who are dissatisfied with how their team works.

To put it plainly, "people problems" are almost always the biggest challenge for entrepreneurial companies, and solving them is transformational.

When you're not getting the most out of your people and you're not all working together to win, that's a sure sign you have underlying problems that need to be addressed. You have team members who don't share your business's fundamental values, or you have many people sitting in the wrong seats of your business. Or more likely, both.

Foundational problems can be ignored for only so long. They penetrate deep into a company's culture, eventually creating chaos, a state of complete disorder and confusion. Even when you manage to escape total chaos, problems on your team still create tremendous amounts of wasted human energy and lost productivity.

But there are a few companies that manage to escape this "people" trap. What they all have in common is this: an intentional culture. *Intentional* meaning something created with purpose and constructed deliberately. And *culture* being defined as the attitudes and behaviors characteristic to your company.

What can an intentional culture do for your business?

Take a minute to imagine your business where the whole team, every single member, shares your Core Values (your company's established cultural norms, behaviors, and beliefs). They fit the company like a glove and embody all the behaviors you value most.

Every customer feels those Core Values in every interaction they have with one of your people. That happens naturally because your people live and breathe those values.

Not only does each person on your team do their job well, but also they're self-motivated and self-managing. The team wakes up in the morning wanting to do their jobs, and they all have the experience, knowledge, time, and skill to get it done.

Word then gets out about how great it is to work at your company. You have a line of people waiting at the door eager to come work for you. You never have to worry if you'll find people. The right people are drawn to your organization based on the culture you've carefully imagined and made reality. That's what an *intentional and healthy* culture looks like. Whether you employ a hundred people or five, this is what your business should strive for consistently.

Of course, what we just painted is a utopia, a perfect vision where every single team member is aligned with your purposeful culture. But we're also realists. Absolute perfection isn't possible when dealing with people.

However, it *is* realistic to get *most* of your people in the right seats in your business, a seat that they get, want, and have the capacity for. In our experience, if you can get to 80 percent or more of your people thriving inside an intentional culture, you *will* get everything you want from your business.

You'll love your team. You'll love what you do. You'll make the money you want to make. And along the way, you'll make a dent in the universe and have time to pursue other passions. Those are the rewards of this journey.

But it's time to take a step back for a moment and see where you are currently. If you paused right now and took a minute to think about your entire team of people—from leadership to the entry-level—what comes to mind? Be completely open and honest with yourself. As Dan Sullivan, co-founder of Strategic Coach® says, all progress starts by telling the truth. You'll gain no benefit from this book if you aren't first honest with yourself.

> **Note:** You'll want to have a journal by your side and something to write with to capture your Issues List and To-Dos throughout the chapters. This will ensure you realize the full value from this book.

Is your company a well-oiled machine? A business where everyone rows in the same direction? Do your people share a common set of Core Values? Are they all focused on a common vision that forms the foundation of what your company is truly about?

No?

Then it's time to admit you don't have an intentional culture. You can take heart in the fact that you're far from alone.

The following is a chart to get you thinking about the culture of your business. Most companies fall somewhere in the lower two quadrants (Chaotic Culture, Happy Accident) or in the upper left quadrant (Command and Control):

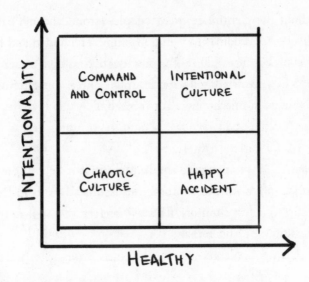

No matter where you currently fall on this chart, the goal is to build a team that puts you in the upper right quadrant (Intentional Culture) and keeps you there. That culture should perfectly reflect your vision of how you want to show up in the world. When you do it right, what you build will be scalable and enduring well beyond you. Let's go through each of the four culture types.

A Happy Accident culture is just that. Your culture is great, but you didn't build it on purpose. Maybe you hired your brother and your cousin and your best friend. You have a great relationship and are crushing it. However, you know that if you add any more people, it will destroy your culture, and so you're afraid. If you're currently living in a Happy Accident culture, that's lucky, but luck is more likely to turn to quicksand than a solid foundation. When adversity hits (and it always does), you cannot count on resiliency, and things can fall apart extremely quickly. Ultimately, a Happy Accident culture doesn't stand the test of time and cannot scale as your company grows.

Even more problematic are cultures in the Command and Control quadrant. This is a kind of intentional culture, but it's built around fear and control exerted by one person, or a small group on the Leadership Team. The tone of the entire business is usually rife with gossip, high turnover, and scared people. People are treated like interchangeable parts. A Command and Control culture is transactional and not particularly relational. It doesn't last.

The final and most unhappy quadrant is Chaotic Culture in the lower left. If you and your business are there, we don't need to explain the pain. You already know how unproductive, miserable, unpredictable, and unhealthy it feels to live there.

EOS is a system for managing human energy. Imagine your business with the people (arrows) in your business pulling in different directions. You may have pockets of people who are bought into your vision and are rowing in the same direction, but too many others are pointing in random directions. The goal of an intentional culture is to get all the arrows pointing in the same direction.

THE HUMAN ENERGY MODEL

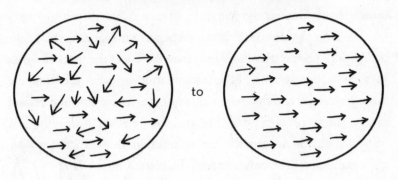

to

Having an unhealthy culture isn't just about the human misery it causes. It also has a massive impact on the bottom line.

According to a study by the Engagement Institute cited in *Forbes* magazine, disengaged employees collectively cost companies between $450 and $550 billion a year in lost productivity. That's the equivalent of lighting ten million high-end luxury cars on fire.

Gallup® polls have shown consistently that only about one-third of US employees are engaged in their work, and an incredible 15 percent are *actively disengaged* and are a toxic cancer in their organizations. These numbers fluctuate slightly over time, but never move much. It should probably come as no surprise that many who report being disengaged also report being poorly managed.

Besides damage to the bottom line, there are also huge hidden costs of a culture filled with disengaged employees. Start with the fact that your people are the biggest catalysts for new employees wanting to come work for you.

Ask yourself how long it takes to find good people when you need to hire. Finding that right person is a huge challenge for most businesses. Wouldn't it be better, smoother, and easier if your current employees and customers sent you constant referrals to people who *want* to work for your company?

Then there's turnover. When your people are spending their days in jobs with people they don't love, they'll leave at the first offer that pays them slightly more. People aren't motivated by money alone; it only becomes a factor when there's no other compelling reason to stay. All of this is incredibly costly in real dollars. According to a study done by the Center for American Progress, the cost of replacing a team member can be over 200 percent of their salary.

Imagine for a moment if you instead had a majority of team members who were actively engaged. If most of them felt clarity, purpose, and total connection with the vision and Core Values of the business they worked for. If they all felt valued and appreciated for their role fulfilling that vision. How much more productive and happier and fulfilled would everyone be?

How much happier could every individual be if they could bring their own unique talents to their jobs and felt great doing it? What could that do for your bottom line? And how much less stressful and more joy-filled could your own life be?

Most employee surveys rank feeling valued, appreciated, and connected to the purpose of the business as more important than anything else in the workplace.

Without a doubt, strengthening and getting the people part right is one of the hardest things to do. It's definitely the messiest. It's just so *human*, often filled with emotion, friction, and misunderstandings. Business owners spin their wheels looking for a way to get their team to play nice and for everyone to "just do their jobs."

But the wheel spinning can stop if you're willing to go on a journey to get this right. It will pay off in ways that will amaze, delight, and inspire you and your competitors.

The great news is that you *can* get it right. The People Component of your business does not have to always remain a mystery. It *is* solvable.

The mindsets, methods, and strategies of building and sustaining a fantastic team are here in this book. When you apply them, it will be transformative for your business and open up the possibility to live the life you dreamed of when you first started as a budding entrepreneur in the making.

We can say that confidently because the concepts and tools in this book are proven to work in real-world settings again and again. They're drawn from the EOS created by founder Gino Wickman. EOS to date has helped tens of thousands of businesses by teaching them to improve the Six Key Components of an organization: Vision, People, Data, Issues, Process, and Traction. This book is all about strengthening *your* People Component.

OVERVIEW OF THE EOS BUSINESS OPERATING SYSTEM

EOS is a simple way of operating a business. It's a complete system, full of timeless concepts and simple, practical tools that help owners and leaders get what they want from their businesses. Through painstaking study and years of trial and error, Gino Wickman discovered how to help Leadership Teams resolve the hundreds of common issues facing an entrepreneurial company.

What Gino found was that each and every common issue was caused by weakness in Vision, People, Data, Issues,

Process, and Traction—what we call the Six Key Components of any business, as illustrated in the EOS Model.

Whether implementing the EOS Tools and concepts on their own or with the aid of an EOS Implementer, Leadership Teams follow a Proven Process to strengthen each of these Six Key Components.

A strong **Vision** Component means everyone in the organization is 100 percent on the same page with where the company is going and exactly how it plans to get there. A strong **People** Component means you've clearly defined what a "great person" means in your unique business and you're great at attracting and retaining them (the topic of this book). A strong **Data** Component means you're running your business on a handful of numbers that give you an absolute pulse on your business, predict future results, and help you make better, faster decisions.

A company with a strong **Issues** Component can solve issues as they arise and make them go away forever, rather than letting them linger for weeks, months, and sometimes even years. A strong **Process** Component is about getting the most important things in your business done the right and best way every time. And finally, a strong **Traction** Component is about instilling discipline and accountability at all levels of the organization so that, everywhere you look, everyone is executing on your vision day in and day out.

The journey to implement EOS is a journey to strengthen *all* Six Key Components. Many leaders mistakenly believe that they can solve all the issues in their business just by working on one or two of them (including People), but we know from experience that becoming 80 percent strong or better in each of the Six Key Components will help you run a truly great business. To get a clear picture of your organizational strength in each of the Six Key Components, visit organizationalcheckup.com.

You can also learn more about EOS by reading *Traction: Get a Grip on Your Business* by Gino Wickman.

There's no need to be an EOS expert to gain value from this book, but those who'd like to learn more can visit eosworldwide.com. To be sure, readers unfamiliar with EOS will still understand and benefit from the concepts and tools in the pages that follow.

All six components matter, of course. But a strong argument can be made that the People Component is foundational to all others. Every other Key Component is executed by your team, so the People Component becomes the driver of all the rest. You can't get what you want from your business without great people.

The Process Component? Implemented by your people. Data Component? Analyzed and made actionable by people. Issues Component? Solved by your team. We could go on, but you get the idea: whatever business you're in, you're also without a doubt in the people business. All five other key components are used to organize and harness the amazing human energy that comes from a great People Component.

Mastering the People Component will have tons of measurable benefits for your business, but bottom-line gains aren't all of it. There are other huge rewards that are less tangible but no less real.

You can look forward to your work life every day with less stress and more joy. You'll reach the point where you have complete confidence that your team can deal with conflict and obstacles, and do it productively. When you develop your people, your freedom skyrockets because your entire team is pointed upward in the same direction, taking you to new heights.

As you implement the concepts outlined in this book, you'll foster a culture of curious and passionate people pursuing mastery, autonomy, and purpose who take personal initiative and accountability in advancing your company's vision. And this will go deeper than just a handful of people on your Leadership Team. Get the People Component right, and a new reality can take hold from top to bottom. Every member all throughout your organization can have the opportunity for more fulfillment and growth.

Okay, but . . .

If that's an achievable vision, why is the reality at so many workplaces so different? In other words, why did 82 percent of companies tell us that they were not getting the most out of their people and were not working together to win before working with EOS?

We've never heard a single entrepreneur say, "I'm starting this business to fulfill my dream of chronic stress for myself and to provide an unhappy workplace where my employees can trade a paycheck for putting up with a chaotic and miserable environment." If it's not the aim, where does dysfunction come from?

In the EOS experience working with thousands of entrepreneurs, the story varies in certain details, but it usually goes something like this:

You start a business, and in the early days, there are a million things that need to get done and very few people to do all of them (sometimes just one). It's a "hair-on-fire" environment. It's all action, action, action, and figure out how to get it done—now.

Growth happens. You need to bring on more people. *Fast.*

This creates a tendency to fall into the trap of WBS—Warm Body Syndrome. The first person you can find with a pulse and meets the bare minimum requirements is hired. Or maybe their only qualification is that they're a friend or family member. Or they're the right person, but you hire them and say, "Good luck, buddy," and spend no time onboarding them, training them, managing them, or making sure they share your vision and Core Values. The flip side is, if you're an employee, you take the highest paying job without regard to culture, and you end up working in a business you aren't a fit for.

The question of whether this person is a good fit with your overall company—and especially its values—rarely gets asked. When you have a lot of fires to put out, the first person who tells you they can hold a fire hose is welcomed aboard.

Plus, at that early stage of your venture, you watch every penny. If you can hire someone for a little less, you do. Completely understandable, but it also plants the wrong seed: people become a commodity, not an investment. As a company grows, that seed will turn out to bear the wrong kind of fruit.

Even when money isn't necessarily the issue, sometimes it just comes down to grabbing the first available person. As they often say in sports, the number one skill is availability. You might hire people for the simple fact that you're desperate to hire someone, and cousin Charlie happens to be available.

The ramifications of all these decisions accumulate as time passes. Your business continues to grow. You feel some danger signs with your team. Even people who you thought were great aren't cutting it anymore. Maybe one of your top salespeople seems to be driving conflicts that cause people to leave. But you can't get rid of a top salesperson, right?

And this other person, she's the only one who can do the accounting. Sure, this person seems to be a ringleader in complaining about every new company initiative and seems to poison other attitudes, but who would keep the books if you let her go? You feel handcuffed because no one else has been trained. So much energy and productivity are sucked out of the organization by people like this. Everyone around them is distracted by the gossip and toxicity, and overall team health and morale suffers.

There's also that difficult conversation that you should have with your marketing manager about his lack of follow-through on a regular basis, but that will be a tough meeting. You plan on getting to it, but there are many other things going on right now, and so somehow it never gets prioritized. Ten years later, they continue to underperform, and your company stagnates.

Still, in spite of all these problems on the team, the overall trajectory of the business continues to go up, and growth covers all sins. The red flags are ignored and sometimes go unrecognized. Many entrepreneurs cling to some kind of vague hope that "all these people problems" will one day go away. But hope isn't a strategy, which becomes painfully obvious when things change.

As Warren Buffett has said, "Only when the tide goes out do you discover who's been swimming naked." And the tide always eventually recedes. The nonstrategy of hope whispers in your ear that when that day comes, you and your team will rise to the occasion. But that isn't true. You'll fall to the lowest level of your preparation.

And eventually, it happens. The tide goes out. Maybe it was due to a downturn in your industry or the economy. Maybe you lost your biggest client, and you weren't paying attention to customer-concentration risk. Maybe it's a global pandemic. Maybe your competitors are performing better. Or your organization has simply hit the ceiling and what used to work isn't working any longer. Whatever the reason, the downturn continues, and the urgency of your people problems can no longer be ignored.

Now you're no longer hitting your numbers, your customers are complaining, or the business is stagnating, and you're beginning to panic. The growth and profit that covered all sins is gone. Now what? Everything that you ignored in the past now comes rising to the top and can't be pushed aside any longer.

It's at this point that many business leaders also realize that what started out as their entrepreneurial dream now feels a lot more like a burden than a passion. Many team members seem to do their own thing, even if it isn't best serving the company. They might change their behavior in the very short term after a talk with them, but pretty soon it goes right back to like it was before. They still don't share your Core Values, and they often fail to get the job done the way it should be done.

We've also seen many circumstances where a business owner is forced to jump back into the weeds of the day-to-day business to handle something that should never be the responsibility of a leader. They're not diving into the details for a heroic ego boost to "save the day"; they're doing it because they're the best person for the job. This is a sure sign that you don't have the Right People in the Right Seats.

WHAT DO WE MEAN BY SEATS?

To strengthen the People Component in your business, we use two tools or disciplines, Right People and Right Seats. Right People are people who share your Core Values, of course, and Right Seats are people who Get it, Want it, and have the Capacity to do their jobs really well. The Accountability Chart is the tool we use for that. It's a simple tool that shows each person's seat name and the five major roles that they're expected to deliver to the business.

▌ACCOUNTABILITY CHART™

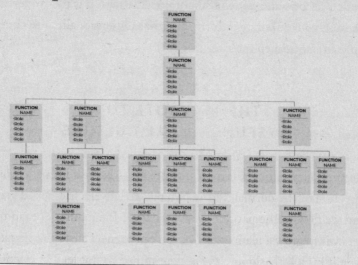

As Steve Jobs once said, "It doesn't make sense to hire smart people and tell them what to do; we hire smart people so they can tell us what to do." If you feel like you have to jump in, either you aren't leading and managing well, or you've made a hiring mistake.

All this makes an entrepreneur wonder if they're truly running a business or it's running them.

The scenario we just painted will likely have some differences from the exact surface facts of your own business. Maybe you're still growing like gangbusters but are stressed out by the dysfunction of your team. Maybe you love a lot of your team, but you see that they don't always work together well to solve problems productively.

Whatever the specifics of your own situation, the commonality for many businesses is this: you wake up one day and realize you've built a chaotic and haphazard culture. The reason is no mystery; it's because your culture was formed without intentionality. It's time to up your game in culture building.

THE ANTIDOTE TO A DYSFUNCTIONAL CULTURE

Business expert Jim Rohn once wrote, "Success lies in the opposite direction of the normal pull." Humans are like electricity and water, and we flow to the path of least resistance. The natural human tendency is to grow a team as fast as you can to meet customer demand, even if it's a little sloppy. You're determined to not let any opportunity pass you by.

Ultimately, though, success with the People Component won't come from following the path of least resistance. It will come from slowing down and having the courage to grow in a way that builds a scalable and enduring culture. Slow is smooth; smooth is fast.

The opposite of the path of least resistance is intentionality. The key principle underlying mastery of the People Component can therefore be summed up at its most basic as this:

If you want a more productive and happier workplace, have courage and dare to build an intentional culture.

As we work with entrepreneurs and they try to break through the ceiling and get to the next level of growth, we see them treating a lot of symptoms instead of addressing the *real* issue at the root. Getting all the Right People in the Right Seats will solve most of the problems, and that's what building a great culture is all about. But it's really hard work. It gets uncomfortable because you have to enter the danger of having a tough conversation. In fact, it's many tough conversations if you're truly serious about changing culture.

Instead of courage, we often hear a lot of excuses for not taking action to fix the culture.

One of those excuses comes in the form of dismissing culture as a secondary concern: "Yes, having a good culture would be a nice thing to have. It'd be great if everyone played nice and all that other good stuff, but that's secondary to my core business concerns."

Translation: Culture building is fine as far as it goes, but not if it threatens to divert the focus from the priority of marketing and delivering a great product or service and serving our customers well. They see building a great culture as a cost, not an investment with a return.

This is thinking of culture as a thin layer on top of a business, perhaps something to make the office more "fun." But culture isn't about adding foosball tables and a smoothie bar. What these leaders don't recognize is that if they were to solve their people issues, they'd build better products and services, they'd sell more, and their customers would be happier. They'd solve their issues at the root so the issues would go away forever, instead of constantly playing Whac-A-Mole, where you solve one issue and another immediately pops up.

Culture isn't an add-on. Intentional culture building goes to the very heart of your business. It's about articulating the values at the core of your business and reshaping the team—through both addition and subtraction—to align with those values and the vision for the organization.

It's about getting the Right People in the Right Seats (a concept first defined by Jim Collins) for both the common good of the company and the fulfillment and development of the unique individuals who make up that company.

Another essential part of a great culture is having clearly defined Core Values that determine the desired behaviors for your people. You'll use these values to make judgments on hiring, firing, reviewing, rewarding, and recognizing your people. (Much more on this in chapter 4.)

It's simply false to believe that the priorities of solving immediate issues are somehow pitted against the priorities of building a culture. In fact, a great culture is the key to growing profits in a more sustainable way. A great culture is an enduring competitive advantage when all your people stay and others can't wait to join your team. Competitors can copy your website or your product, but very few want to do the hard work required to build a culture that wins.

INTENTIONAL CULTURE: WHAT DOES IT TAKE?

If you see the value of growing an intentional culture and its power to fuel sustainable growth, the next obvious question is how to do it.

The long answer to that question is in this book. The keys to mastering the People Component of your business are all right here for the taking (although, of course, you have to act on it). As you begin this journey (or perhaps continue it), we want to share three foundational concepts to set you up for success on the way toward an intentional culture.

FOUNDATIONAL CONCEPT 1: BE INTENTIONAL

The subtitle of this book is "Dare to Build an Intentional Culture" for a reason. If you have a business, you already have built a culture. It's just that chances are your culture may be somewhat disorganized and may not be particularly purposeful. If it lacks purpose, it could be toxic, or at least could be moving in that direction.

Your culture might even be great, but not intentional (that's the Happy Accident quadrant). You're good for now, but will it be sustainable? Is it scalable? Highly unlikely if you aren't being intentional.

We'll share the tools that are required to build one purposely, but this only works if you and your Leadership Team throw out the old playbook and fully commit to a culture defined by intentionality.

Many times, business leaders make the mistake of ignoring the role of intentionality and instead believe that trying to "do more" will fix everything. In her book *Contagious Culture*, Anese Cavanaugh discusses this very problem:

"Organizations often think the way to optimize their culture or fix their problems is to do more. Simply more. They'll have meetings and initiatives, seek out feedback training and leadership skills building, hold strategy sessions to 'address this thing' and off-site events to build trust and create the culture they want. And then they'll put people together in a room to do more of the same—more doing."

A new employee handbook or sending out another engagement survey will not produce results. These types of things may have value, but they will most definitely not help you build an enduring culture.

Cavanaugh acknowledges that while some of this can be good, it misses the larger point. She says when you fail to address how people's "being" aligns with the company culture, lots and lots of potential is wasted. Any gains of the "just-do-more" approach will not be sustainable. She concludes:

"This is ironic because when we focus more on intention and 'being' and how people show up together, the doing becomes much easier, and we don't have to work that hard in the first place. So what is it that creates the most impact in how people show up? It's the **intentions** they hold, **the energy they bring** into the room, and **how alive they feel**. It's their presence." [Emphasis added].

Ultimately, you have to build your company on purpose. You need to discover and define the following for your business:

- Core Values (cultural norms, behaviors, beliefs)
- Core Focus (purpose, cause, passion, and niche)
- 10-Year Target (where you're going five to thirty years out)
- Marketing Strategy (who are your ideal customers and how you uniquely serve them)
- 3-Year Picture (what does your world look like three short years from now)
- 1-Year Plan (three to seven goals for the year)
- Rocks (ninety-day priorities)

- Issues List (issues, opportunities, roadblocks, ideas that need to be solved in ninety-plus days)
- Accountability Chart (roles, teams structure, the seats)
- Scorecards (KPIs, metrics, dashboards)
- Meetings (how you meet, when you meet, why you meet, with specific outcomes)

The answers to the above list will form the heart of your Five Foundational Tools, including the Vision/Traction Organizer or V/TO, a crucial EOS tool for creating an intentional culture. You'll learn more about it in the next chapter.

FOUNDATIONAL CONCEPT 2: COURAGE MATTERS

In our experience working with thousands of entrepreneurs, the biggest barrier to building an intentional culture is a lack of courage. It's a failure to systematically deal with people problems head-on throughout the organization. Once a business starts getting clear on accountability and values, it becomes harder to ignore who isn't aligned with the organization.

And, honestly, that can feel a little scary, as in "Wait, does this mean I am going to have to fire my cousin?" or "Does this mean one of my top salespeople is a wrong fit and also has to go—how will I make up that revenue?" or "I love that employee. I have to have the hard conversation that his current seat is too big for him?" or "My best product designer is retiring, how am I going to replace her?"

We get it. It can feel frightening to start rocking the boat, because maybe it will capsize. But that boat is probably already taking on water because of inaction. It may be time to find some new captains and crew members and a bigger, better boat. As speaker, author, and philosopher George Addair says, "Everything you've ever wanted is sitting on the other side of fear."

And take heart in this. As you begin the journey of *daring* to build an intentional culture, know that EOS has proven methods, strategies, and completely road-tested tools to get you where you want to go. What you learn in this book *does* work. When the implementation feels scary or hard, it can be helpful to remember a happier, more productive workplace awaits you on the other side.

FOUNDATIONAL CONCEPT 3: INVEST THE TIME (AND MONEY)

Building an intentional culture is serious work, and it isn't something that can be accomplished in a thirty- or even ninety-day window. You can't replace everyone in one day. That would be a painful and unproductive day. Plan on a minimum of about twelve to eighteen months to begin to see the changes pay off, and sometimes even longer. If you can make one great people move per quarter, in the long run, you'll get the results you want.

In other words: If you're going to treat this like the next flavor-of-the-month initiative, you might as well close the book now.

Expect to weather some early turnover as the wrong people leave. That's okay. The "wrong" people don't share your culture or aren't capable of meeting your expectations anyway. Expect change—sometimes upheaval—as you work through getting the Right People in the Right Seats. Prepare for serious debates on Core Values and resistance from pockets within your company.

Entrepreneurs have that quality of always reaching for more, of wanting to find fresh, innovative ideas that help them grow as individuals, and of helping their companies grow. This is a great quality—in some ways, it's at the heart of the entrepreneur's ability to take risks and continue to push themselves to be better. But it's a double-edged sword. It cuts back the wrong way when it turns into chasing the next shiny object. The search for "more and better" or "the silver bullet" splinters and becomes a lack of consistency and focus.

If you introduce a different flavor every month too many times to your team, they will start to view you as the Leader Who Cried Wolf trying some new management fad you'll never stick with. Then they tune you out.

Choosing a new "People" initiative every month is like falling for a fad diet. Having the courage to build an intentional culture is like deciding to make a change to a healthier *lifestyle*. The only way this works is to commit to an intentional culture and make lasting changes. The key is to align your entire company around the care and feeding of each employee for their (and your) growth. It isn't for the faint of heart.

THE PAYOFF

Think about your business. What couldn't you accomplish if all twenty out of twenty or seventy-five out of seventy-five of your people were rowing in the same direction fully engaged? You'd be unstoppable! As messy and human as the process can be, when *you* commit to the methods, tools, and strategies we outline in the following chapters, it works.

Lives will be changed, and businesses can become much more resilient during downturns and other shocks to the system. It won't be all roses, rainbows, and lollipops along the way, but the payoffs are enormous, both in profits and happiness.

What lies ahead is a work environment where people feel valued and appreciated, and a culture where the goal is to get all the human energy on your team pointed in the same direction. Jim Goodnight, cofounder of SAS Institute, put it succinctly: "Treat employees like they make a difference, and they will."

Your organization will begin to attract and keep all the right employees who will greatly contribute to your mutual success. You'll have a line of employees waiting to work for you. How beautiful would that be?

WHAT IS THE EOS LIFE?

It can be defined by five key points: doing what you love, with people you love, making a huge difference, while being compensated appropriately, and with time for other passions. In its most ideal form, this is what these five points look like:

1. **Doing What You Love** means that you spend your working time doing only the activities you love to do and are great at doing. The actions that give you unlimited energy and excitement.
2. **With People You Love** means that everyone in your life—your coworkers, customers, vendors, friends, and family—are people you enjoy being around and who uplift you.
3. **Making a Huge Difference** means that you're having the exact impact that you want to have on the world.

4. **Being Compensated Appropriately** means making as much money as you want by providing value to others, helping them get what they want.

5. **With Time for Other Passions** means that you spend the amount of time you want on your passions, those things outside of work that you enjoy and give you energy.

What does building an intentional culture have to do with living The EOS Life?

We will explore this more fully in chapter 10, but the short answer is: When you build an intentional culture, you hold the keys to living The EOS Life and your own customized version of it.

Building an intentional culture can have a massive impact on the quality of the owner's life. Donna Hanson, owner of Burgoon Company, an industrial supply company in Texas, told her Certified EOS Implementer Randy McDougal this: "My personal and professional best is the company is running so much more smoothly, and I am not so distracted and anxious checking on things. The most important part of this is that when I am with my grandchildren, I am actually with them. I disengage from the business and truly enjoy the time focused on them."

Donna was not the only one who recognized the difference. Her daughter Emily Marks, a brand-new member of the Leadership Team, heard her mom say this, and added her own comment: "Well, Mom, I haven't told you yet, but last week my two sons said how much more fun it is to be with you. They said you're listening to them and so fun to be with."

That's what building a great enduring culture is all about. There are the real-life payoffs ahead. We can promise you big challenges. But if you have the courage to build an intentional culture, you'll get even bigger rewards. Do you dare begin?

REFLECTION QUESTIONS

In our work with business owners, we find resistance to dealing with the People Component until economic pressures, frustration, misery, or some other strong motivator forces change. Building an intentional culture won't happen until you're all in. Read these questions and answer honestly. If you cannot give an emphatic yes to most or all of these, you're not ready.

1. Do you recognize that your current culture is holding you back from getting what you want from your business?

2. Are you willing to take responsibility for creating and leading every aspect of your culture (and that doesn't mean delegating to human resources)?

3. Are you willing to do what it takes to become your best and demand the best from yourself and your company and make all the necessary tough decisions?

4. Do you believe you and your team deserve a culture that wins in any environment and economy?

5. Are you willing and have the courage to be open, honest, and vulnerable to build an intentional and enduring culture?

To go deeper on assessing your current culture, go to **eosworldwide.com/people-book** and take the Culture Checkup.

• • • • • • • • • • • • • • •

"Living a life I didn't dare dream..."

For fifteen years, I tried to run the company. I didn't have the language then to know I was trying to be both the Integrator (president) and the Visionary (CEO).

I've always been good at attracting smart people and giving them room to do their jobs, but it wasn't until we embraced the clarity of the Accountability Chart that the team started reaching their potential.

Four years ago, I handed the reins to our first Integrator. We spent time together weekly for two hours—to build the trust we both needed for this to work well. I needed to know he cared about the people and the organization as deeply as I did as the founder. He needed to be able to trust that he was not going to be fired for making a mistake. He needed to know I was going to give him the freedom to try things, to experiment. To make changes. We knew directional progress was imperative, but perfection wasn't.

Two years into my first Integrator, we supported his dream by making a $250,000 investment in a technology company he was starting and transitioned to a new Integrator who has allowed us to continue our winning trajectory.

We've moved the company from 6 percent to over 24 percent profitability and our eNPS (employee Net Promoter Score) has gone from low forties to our most recent score thirty days ago of a ninety-two.

Letting go of the vine and fully delegating is often complicated by Visionaries since we overestimate our capabilities. We believe we can "train" our Integrators to do a job well that we've never done well ourselves.

The best thing we can do is create a clear vision of the future and get out of the way. In both of my experiences, the most important thing for me to transfer was a clear understanding of how our company values translated into decision-making, pace of change, expectations, and a winning mindset. The mechanics of the job—I knew very little about how to make them successful at that pace. That was what they had to bring to the table.

Today, I'm living a life I didn't dare dream could be possible four years ago. I have flexibility of time to be available for my four girls. I'm home nearly every day when my kids get off the school bus. I have an abundance of financial resources to share with organizations and causes near to our heart. I can go away for a couple of weeks and explore and ski with my family. I can lead vacation Bible school at my church. I have time to support a podcast and newsletter that helps others with similar-size dreams in their hearts. I've purchased and invested in companies that I believe can change the world.

—Tiffany Sauder, CEO and Visionary of Element Three

CHAPTER 2

. . . .

WHAT'S LOVE GOT TO DO WITH IT?

"IF YOU REMOVE LOVE OR TRUTH, IT IS CRUELTY."
—PATRICK LENCIONI

In the previous chapter, we defined culture as "the attitudes and behaviors characteristic to your company."

A definition is a good first step, but then the question is: How accurate are you at recognizing your company's fundamental attitudes and behaviors? Can you see the culture you swim in? It's kind of like the question, "Does a fish know it's wet?" It can be hard to get outside your own day-to-day environment and identify foundational problems.

Seeing clearly in this area is important. If your culture is fundamentally oriented in the wrong direction, you won't be able to sustain any progress in building the team you want.

Think of it this way: you can plan out a garden very carefully and intentionally, but if you try to plant it on rocks, it will never become a healthy garden. However, that same well-planned garden will thrive in rich, healthy soil.

In a similar way, an intentional culture needs the right environment to grow healthily. In business, the right soil is a fundamental orientation toward abundance and love. On the other hand, a company culture heavily pointed in the direction of scarcity and fear is on rocky ground.

This chapter is going to help you take a closer look at your own current culture and diagnose its fundamental orientation. Then we'll show how you can root your culture in the richer soil of abundance and love.

ANALYZING YOUR CULTURE: WHICH WAY IS IT POINTED?

As we touched upon in chapter 1, there are healthy and unhealthy versions of intentional cultures. We often walk into businesses that think their culture is healthy—or at least okay—but we can instantly spot significant problems.

Often those problems reveal themselves in the form of a culture intentionally built on Command and Control. Those companies are no fun to be a part of because people are thought of as tools used to get a job done, not as unique individuals with immense value.

Command and Control cultures are formed because we live in a commoditized world that's hypercompetitive and often fear-based. It's natural in that kind of world for a culture rooted in scarcity and fear to become unhealthy, and sometimes downright toxic.

WHAT'S LOVE GOT TO DO WITH IT?

This is why it's so important to actively choose a different basis for your culture. A healthy intentional culture treats every human as a unique gift, deserving of honor and respect. It consciously creates an environment that allows individuals to grow and flourish and contribute in their own way.

Simply put, an intentional culture is created on the basis of abundance and love and a Command and Control culture is built on scarcity and fear. Abundance and love are in direct contrast to scarcity and fear. Look at this comparison chart and honestly assess which better describes your culture:

ABUNDANCE & LOVE	SCARCITY AND FEAR
POSITIVE	NEGATIVE
OPTIMISTIC	PESSIMISTIC
COLLABORATIVE	COMPETITIVE
LONG-TERM	SHORT-TERM
PROACTIVE	REACTIVE
CONTENTMENT	ANXIETY & STRESS
GRATITUDE	ENTITLEMENT
SELF-WORTH & CONFIDENCE	INADEQUACY & SELF-DOUBT
GENEROSITY	HOARDING

In our journey of guiding and collaborating with businesses, we've discovered that a significant number of them unknowingly lean toward a mindset of scarcity and fear rather than embracing the empowering principles of abundance and love.

Some entrepreneurial businesses are scrappy and want to crush the competition, and sometimes they can't identify what makes them unique in the marketplace, so the only thing they have left is to compete on price. That's the definition of commodity business.

In a competitive landscape where businesses and individuals lack distinctiveness, you and your Leadership Team may inadvertently treat each team member uniformly, as if they were merely cogs in a machine, overlooking their exceptional talents and the valuable contributions they bring to the table. This mindset creates a culture of Command and Control, one that's built on scarcity and fear.

A company that builds its culture on the basis of scarcity and fear typically has high turnover, has difficulty recruiting top talent, never gets the best out of their people, and has razor-thin margins. Their products and services are equally undifferentiated and their customers will leave them for the next lowest price competitor.

We don't want to overstate or oversimplify here. No business is always 100 percent abundant and loving, and no company is ruled by scarcity and fear in every interaction. If you think of it as a continuum...

ABUNDANCE AND LOVE

SCARCITY AND FEAR

Then the key question becomes where is your organization on this continuum? The questions you need to reflect on are the following:

- Where is your business on the continuum right now?
- And which direction are you headed?

So this isn't about perfection. It's about defining your organization's orientation and location on this continuum of scarcity and fear versus abundance and love and recognizing this has a massive impact on how your people experience the business's culture on a day-to-day basis.

Your first reaction may be that your business isn't oriented toward scarcity and fear, and of course that may be true. However, it's worth digging a little deeper. By looking in the mirror and being open and honest, you may become aware that change is necessary.

GOING DEEPER TO DIAGNOSE YOUR CULTURE

Here's one way to begin diagnosing whether fear and scarcity have crept in: Is your business often reactive instead of proactive? For example, do you find your business most often reacts to changes in the industry rather than anticipating or even shaping those trends? Do you find that your team is always reacting to customer issues instead of learning lessons and preventing those issues? Do you especially find that many internal relationships between team members are filled with unresolved conflict? Do you have an us-versus-them mentality? Do your team members talk negatively about your customers, or each other? Is there always a sense of scarcity around resources and playing a zero-sum game?

If you recognize reactivity in your business culture, that's a clue to scarcity and fear.

The fear mindset leads to all kinds of poor decisions. You hire from a place of scarcity, thinking, *I've got to fill this position right now.*

And you end up with an unqualified relative in the position or a new hire who doesn't fit your company's values.

Or you know you should address the people who are in the wrong position in your company, but fear starts talking: *That'll be a messy confrontation. The status quo is manageable. I'll address it later. It's better to have someone in that role rather than an open position.*

Or what about that person who is a star performer who also generates so much negative energy internally that some have left the company because of it? Scarcity and fear say, *But, yeah, how would I ever replace her?*

Let's go one step further and talk about a specific form of scarcity and fear that we see all too often. See if you recognize it at all in your own organization.

SUCK-IT-UP CULTURE ISN'T BRAVE—IT JUST SUCKS

Entrepreneurship isn't for the faint of heart. Starting and growing a business requires grit, resilience, and a willingness to weather setbacks and failures. As the saying goes, "There's no crying in business," and most entrepreneurs would agree that toughness and perseverance are essential qualities for success.

You won't catch us arguing with the need for grit, toughness, stick-to-it-iveness, and occasionally having to do things you don't want to do in order to get important things done. But this helpful toughness often slides into another kind of thinking, something much more destructive.

It somehow becomes okay for people to trudge through day after day, performing a role that does not fit them, and label it toughness.

Just suck it up, right? Sometimes people even start to celebrate a suck-it-up mentality as some sort of honor.

No. Instead, we should be asking things like, *Hey, wait a minute. Is it a good idea to have a business where many employees do something they kind of hate, even if they're competent at it?* And, *Is it smart to have employees who are in roles too big for their capacities and letting them muddle through? Is that good for them, and is it good for the organization?* Is that really how you, yourself, want to live your life, or let your employees live their lives?

Those questions go unasked when there is no clear alternative to fear culture, so the default position becomes "just suck it up" for all concerned. The team member stuck in the wrong position figures they just need to suck it up. Everyone who has to work around them or take up the slack or deal with their unhappiness—they figure they just have to suck it up, too.

This mentality requires more effort, and more effort equates to more stress and less productivity. So not only does it reduce efficiency, but it's also not sustainable. You can address it as soon as it's identified if you ask if each of your people GWC their roles (*get* their roles, *want* their roles, and have the *capacity* for their roles), *or* you can wait until the fire is out of control.

Sometimes in these situations, people manage to convince themselves that sucking it up is brave and heroic—a doing of one's duty. But is it? How many work lives have been wasted with that attitude? How much productivity and creativity lost? How much business growth has been sacrificed while everyone is busy sucking it up?

Perhaps the truly brave and heroic thing is to do something about it. Maybe it's time to take the risk of putting love and abundance at the center of your culture's mindset.

PUTTING THE LOVE IN IT

Love as a word connected to business makes some leaders nervous or uncomfortable. We get it. It sounds a little soft. Emotional. One of those touchy-feely words that's too vague to be helpful.

There is a different way to think about it. The way we're using the word *love* is of course not in the romantic sense. And we aren't talking about standing in a ring around a campfire, singing uplifting songs. All of those can be fine kinds of love, but that's not what we mean.

We're referring to love that has nothing to do with romance. The love we mean is filled with kindness, charity, affectionate regard, and respect between equals. The ancient Greeks referred to this kind of love as *agape* or *philia*.

What we're saying is simply this: for EOS tools to be most effective, the intentional culture you build needs to be rooted in Genuine Care and Concern for one another. We refer to this as *heart-centered leadership*.

This quote from John C. Maxwell sums it up well: "To be an effective leader, you must not only have knowledge and competence, but you must also have empathy and compassion for those you lead." People are more likely to follow and trust a leader who demonstrates Genuine Care and Concern for them.

In the world of EOS, we often express this concept by using the phrase "putting the love in it." Some folks hear that and get worried that it means we encourage injecting more emotion into our work. We get it, and on one level, that's even true.

But here's the deeper truth: putting the love in it is actually a way to take some of the emotion out of the decisions we make so that things run easier and with less friction.

When we're trying to please someone emotionally, it's all too easy to get bogged down in assumptions and fear. But when we're truly seeking to *serve* them—to help them live their best life—we can remove that fear and act with confidence, secure in the knowledge that we're doing the right thing for them. And that's what putting the love in it is all about.

WHAT HEART-CENTERED LEADERSHIP LOOKS LIKE

There are five keys to becoming a business with heart-centered leadership (aka "putting the love in it"):

- LOVE IS A VERB
- GREATER GOOD
- GENUINE CARE AND CONCERN FOR PEOPLE
- AUTHENTICITY
- HUMAN CREATIVE POWER

Before we look at these one by one, understand that, in practice, these aren't stand-alone concepts. They all work together. For example, the amount of authenticity you bring to the other four keys is crucial, or none of the others will work.

Another example: you'll only unleash the full creative power of each team member if you show them genuine care and concern.

All the keys of heart-centered leadership stand or fall together.

LOVE IS A VERB

Behind the idea of putting the love in it is a sincere feeling of wanting what is best for another person. But that feeling can only be truly expressed in concrete and practical actions. Otherwise, the feeling itself becomes meaningless. In short, *love* is a verb. Some examples of when you show love are the following:

- You purchase a software tool that allows your people to automate some of the tedious parts of their job.
- You give a person the budget to hire someone so they can use the Delegate and Elevate tool (more on this tool later).
- You give a team member your total focus and attention during a Quarterly Conversation (more on Quarterly Conversations later).
- You release someone who isn't a good fit or underperforming so they can pursue another position where they feel fulfilled and can make a difference.
- You have the courage to be open and honest with people about what they're doing really well and where they're falling short.
- You genuinely strive to help members of your team reach peaceful resolution.
- You use Clarity Breaks (quiet time to intuitively and instinctively consider what's most important) before meeting with team members so that you give them your best.
- You dig deep and "enter the danger" to truly get to the root of an issue, even, or especially, when it's hard.
- You challenge each other's thinking, putting as much care into your decision-making as possible.

As you can see, love at work should always be practical, active, and proven. It's your daily actions, words, and behavior that determine if you're loving or not.

Love also should come out in tough situations, like those cases when a current team member is the wrong fit for your unique culture. Love in these situations means straightforward honesty. Of course, the person in front of you may not recognize that honesty as loving in that moment. But if they're miserable, you're giving them a chance to find a new path they can't see for themselves. They may come to see that later and thank you for it. Either way, you can only do your part and hope they eventually realize that it was for the best.

We have seen failure in this area again and again—it's one of the most common people issues we help businesses confront. We have seen cases where owners have kept people *for decades* that were not a fit—all to avoid messy emotions. In these cases, emotions aren't really being eliminated—they're just being pushed down and deferred to deal with at a later date. The results are long-term simmering resentments and wasted lives.

As one of our clients said, "We've been dancing around the 'Janet' issue for ten years, so it's a good thing that you finally forced us to make a decision." Most companies have their own "Janet" issue, and the longer it goes, the worse it is for all concerned.

With a heart-centered approach that combines clear values and strong cultural standards, you no longer rely on in-the-moment emotion. Instead, you use those clear standards to define whether a person is both serving their own unique talents and the Greater Good of the company. The standards create the objective measure that allows you to remove a lot of the emotion.

Pastor Randy Gariss, in his book *Freedom from Performing: Grace in an Applause-Driven World*, said, "Nice does not equal kind. Kind equals truth plus grace." This quote emphasizes the idea that being nice, or simply trying to please others, is not the same as being kind. Being truly kind involves a deeper sense of empathy and a real commitment to telling the truth in a loving and compassionate way.

GREATER GOOD

Heart-centered leadership needs a guiding star, a touchstone principle to ultimately determine the lovingness of an action. For a business culture, that measure should be what best serves the Greater Good.

Defining the Greater Good

At EOS Worldwide, our yardstick for how we serve others well is always pursuing the Greater Good of the organization. Here's the simple formula:

$$\text{GREATER GOOD} = \text{EVERY WORD OF THE V/TO}$$
$$\times$$
$$\text{GENUINE CARE AND CONCERN}$$

The V/TO (Vision/Traction Organizer) is a way to boil down your vision into a two-page document that gets your vision out of your head and down on paper. Besides bringing clarity for the Leadership Team, it will also allow everyone else in your organization to see where you want to go.

It ensures that your team is focused and aligned on The 8 Questions of Core Values, Core Focus, Core Target, your Marketing Strategy, 3-Year Picture, 1-Year Plan, Rocks, and Issues list. Your intentional culture needs a clear, precise vision, and the V/TO is the master key for it.

It would be hard to overestimate the importance of a great V/TO! To go deeper on this crucial topic, we recommend *Traction* by Gino Wickman.

The second part of the formula is Genuine Care and Concern, a multiplier to greater good being achieved. It means exactly what it says: that in all your actions, behaviors, and words, you have Genuine Care and Concern for every team member. The formula is simple, but we all fall short in executing it sometimes. All of this is just another way to express putting the love in it.

A common objection is that the Greater Good seems like it could often be in tension with what is loving and best for each individual. What if what is best for a team member is in conflict with what is best for the company?

Before becoming a Certified EOS Implementer, Josh Kwasny was part of a team that was running on EOS. He answers this objection with a story from those days:

"During this time, we had to let go of an employee, and it was a difficult decision. However, we used the tools provided by EOS to ensure that everyone was clear on the reasons why we were making that hard decision. To our surprise, this former employee later returned to thank us for caring enough to be honest. Our decision to let him go had been a wake-up call for him, and he had since moved on to a new company where he's thriving. This experience showed me the power of being transparent and honest in business. Even when tough decisions have to be made, using a system like EOS can help ensure that everyone understands the reasons why, which can lead to better outcomes for all involved."

VISION/TRACTION ORGANIZER™

ORGANIZATION NAME: _____

EOS MODEL®

VISION

CORE VALUES	1. 2. 3. 4. 5.
CORE FOCUS™	Purpose/Cause/Passion: Our Niche:
10-YEAR TARGET™	

MARKETING STRATEGY	Target Market/"The List":
	
	Three Uniques™: 1.
	                           2.
	                           3.
	Proven Process:
	
	Guarantee:

3-YEAR PICTURE™

Future Date:
Revenue:
Profit:
Measurables:
What Does It Look Like?

· · · · · · · · · · · ·

VISION/TRACTION ORGANIZER™

ORGANIZATION NAME: _____

EOS MODEL®

TRACTION

1-YEAR PLAN	ROCKS	ISSUES LIST
Future date: Revenue: Profit: Measurables:	Future date: Revenue: Profit: Measurables:	
Goals for the Year	**Rocks for the Quarter** **Who**	
1. _____	1. _____	1. _____
2. _____	2. _____	2. _____
3. _____	3. _____	3. _____
4. _____	4. _____	4. _____
5. _____	5. _____	5. _____
6. _____	6. _____	6. _____
7. _____	7. _____	7. _____
		8. _____
		9. _____
		10. _____
		Prioritize • Identify • Discuss • Solve

Steve Jobs has a similar take from the time when he was famously fired from Apple: "I'm pretty sure none of this [referring to Apple's extreme success] would have happened if I hadn't been fired from Apple. It was awful-tasting medicine, but I guess the patient needed it. Sometimes life hits you in the head with a brick. Don't lose faith. I'm convinced that the only thing that kept me going was that I loved what I did. You've got to find what you love."

The truth is that serving both the Greater Good and individuals doesn't need to be opposed or mutually exclusive. If the person doesn't fit the values of the organization or doesn't have the capacity to do their job, it isn't in their best long-term interests to stay. Not confronting the issue could allow them to waste their work life. Being honest allows them a chance to find the place where they fit.

This is also not just about people who can't perform well in their current roles. Many people get caught up in the "excellence trap," where they refuse to admit they don't love what they're doing. They're so afraid of failing that they perform at a very high level, but deep down, they're miserable.

As a leader, recognize that there's another factor here. You have more than just one person to consider. It's stressful for those who are aligned with your culture to fight the drag of those not aligned. The culture of the business has to be cultivated with the Greater Good kept firmly in mind, or there may be no business for anyone to work for.

GENUINE CARE AND CONCERN FOR PEOPLE

Another key concept in creating a culture with abundance and love at its core is to make sure you're treating people in relational terms, not transactional terms. On a profit and loss statement, payroll is a cost. But that's bookkeeping. To get culture right, think of people as relationships to invest in. You should be thinking of all your people as investments, not costs to be reduced and eliminated.

When you appreciate someone or something, the value grows. You nurture your people and your relationships with them in hopes that they grow and increase in value over time.

Do you show Genuine Care and Concern for your people? This is definitely a leadership issue. It starts with the owners and Visionaries and Integrators. The relationships and mindsets coming from the top set the tone and actions for the rest of the leadership and on down through the organization.

If everyone sees the owner consistently cultivating care and concern, they'll follow suit. But no amount of talk about intentional culture will overcome an owner who says, "Do as I say, not as I do."

AUTHENTICITY

Some leaders care quite naturally. Others come to the insight slowly, but then become galvanized when they see the power of it. And others struggle with ever getting it.

Before joining EOS Worldwide, one of us knew a CEO who made it a point to travel from cubicle to cubicle engaging with employees every morning. He believed that small talk was the key to building rapport. However, his interactions felt forced and interrupted the employees' daily routines. It seemed he was just following a script he'd read somewhere about effective leadership.

In another attempt to foster a positive work environment, this same CEO approved a budget for department managers to treat their team members to a birthday lunch. Though well-intentioned, things took a turn for the worse when the CEO reprimanded a manager for leaving a 20 percent tip instead of the company-standard 15 percent.

The birthday lunch, which was meant to nurture team spirit and appreciation, turned into a cold, transactional issue. The CEO's lack of self-awareness hindered his ability to authentically connect with his employees. While his intentions were good, the execution fell short, undermining the very purpose of these initiatives.

In situations like this, EOS can help leaders stay focused on their Core Values and goals while fostering genuine, positive relationships with their team members.

Little things count. Daily actions matter, people notice, and it accumulates as do deposits in an emotional bank account. Details are a key part of building a culture.

In *How to Be a Great Boss* by Gino Wickman and René Boer, they emphasize that when it comes to Leadership, Management, and Accountability (LMA), your personal style or personality isn't the determining factor in being an effective leader. Whether you're tough, easygoing, or somewhere in between, the key to becoming a great leader and manager lies in authentically caring for your team members and prioritizing their well-being.

HUMAN CREATIVE POWER

A true leader wants to honor and serve that uniqueness in everyone. What a fantastic goal for any entrepreneur: to create an organization with a culture that helps as many people get what they want by being who they truly are.

In many ways, this is where much of the power of an intentional culture comes from: unleashing the talents, abilities, and "superpowers" of each and every team member. It's truly an awe-inspiring force.

The best way to access and unleash each team member's power is with the concept of a Personal Core Focus.

A Personal Core Focus highlights an individual's unique combination of talents, passions, and strengths, which drive personal and professional success. You can think of it as the purpose, passion, and niche of the individual.

UNDERSTANDING PERSONAL CORE FOCUS

Personal Core Focus, core competencies, innate talents, personal genius, or sometimes referred to as Unique Ability® (a concept of Dan Sullivan, co-founder of Strategic Coach), highlights an individual's unique combination of talents, passions, and strengths, which drive personal and professional success.

It can be useful to see the similarities between a Personal Core Focus and the Core Focus section of the V/TO. The Core Focus in the V/TO defines the purpose/cause/passion of the business, and defines what the business is better at doing than any other organization in the world. In a comparable way, the Personal Core Focus defines for the individual their purpose/cause/passion, and what their unique talents and competencies allow them to do better than anyone else.

By understanding and embracing your Personal Core Focus, you can align your daily activities with your innate abilities, leading to greater satisfaction and success in your personal and professional lives.

When you identify Personal Core Focus, you can concentrate on the areas where people excel and are passionate, allowing them to make better decisions and achieve goals more effectively. This self-awareness helps you focus on your strengths, develop your skills, and pursue opportunities that align with your unique abilities.

To harness the power of Personal Core Focus, you should do the following:

STEP 1: COMPLETE YOUR LAUNDRY LIST

Take out a journal or something to write on. We recommend handwriting. It's been scientifically proven to increase creativity, focus, and learning over typing, but you choose. Think about all the activities you've done over the last few weeks or months. List everything out big and small. Take a look at your calendar and your To-Do List if you need some prompting.

Your list will look something like this:

```
            THE LAUNDRY LIST
    - CHECKING EMAIL
    - TEAM MEETINGS
    - MOWING THE LAWN
    - SALES CALLS
    - WRITING PROPOSALS
    - RECORDING YOUTUBE VIDEOS
    - CLEANING THE HOUSE
    - GROCERY SHOPPING
    - BOOKKEEPING
    - REVIEWING FINANCIALS
    - QA REVIEW OF PRODUCTS
    - DEBUGGING SOFTWARE
    - DESIGNING MARKETING EMAIL
    - SCHEDULING DOCTOR'S
         APPOINTMENTS
```

STEP 2: CATEGORIZE YOUR LAUNDRY LIST IN THE DELEGATE AND ELEVATE TOOL

Now that you have your Laundry List, get in touch with the way each of the activities make you feel. Do they give you energy or drain you? Do they excite you, or do you procrastinate on them? Take out your journal and categorize each item in one of four quadrants (see below).

Love/Great are those activities that give you energy and you're passionate about. You can't believe you get paid to do them. **Like/ Good** are those things that you do like, but you don't have endless energy for. You're excellent at doing the work. It's like cake—we like cake, but you can have too much cake. **Don't Like/Good** are things you've built up a level of competence for over time. You're good at them, but you push them off as long as you can because you've grown tired of doing these types of activities. They're boring and annoying. **Don't Like/Not Good** are those things that you do that you really shouldn't be doing. They drain you, tick you off, and worst of all, don't get productive results when you do them.

When you're finished it should look something like this:

DELEGATE AND ELEVATE

LOVE/GREAT	LIKE/GOOD
- SALES CALLS - RECORDING VIDEOS - TEAM MEETINGS	- WRITING PROPOSALS - MOWING THE LAWN
DON'T LIKE/GOOD	**DON'T LIKE/NOT GOOD**
- REVIEWING FINANCIALS - GROCERY SHOPPING - DEBUGGING SOFTWARE - QA REVIEW - SCHEDULING DOCTOR'S APPOINTMENTS	- CHECKING EMAIL - BOOKKEEPING - CLEANING THE HOUSE

STEP 3: DISCOVER YOUR PASSIONS AND STRENGTHS

Get out your journal and draw a line through the page. On one side, list "Passions" and on the other "Strengths." Reflect on what you listed using the Delegate and Elevate tool. Write down what is at the core of the activities you put in the **Love/Great** quadrant. Why do these things light you up? What is the common element underlying these activities?

Think of your *passions* this way. They're the things you did as a child that most of us stopped doing as we got older. For example, maybe your six-year-old self was a great debater, but you stopped because it didn't make you a lot of friends. But the reality is you're still passionate about debating the finer points of the impact of (for example) artificial intelligence on the world. Or maybe you were passionate about being outside when you were young, and could always be found with friends in the woods collaborating on a project to take over the world. It's possibly a passion you still have but no longer honor.

Then there are *strengths*. There are quite a few tools or assessments to help you "know thyself." We recommend Kolbe A™ Index Instinct Test, Gallup®, Clifton StrengthsFinder®, PRINT®, and Patrick Lencioni's The 6 Types of Working Genius® Assessment. These assessments are great at helping you get clear on your strengths, the things you're great at and what others rely on you for.

Your completed passions and strengths should look something like this:

CORE STRENGTHS AND PASSIONS

PASSIONS	STRENGTHS
- HELPING PEOPLE GET WHAT THEY WANT	- COMMUNICATING
- INSPIRING PEOPLE TO TAKE ACTION	- PRESENTING
	- SELLING

STEP 4: CREATE YOUR PERSONAL CORE FOCUS

Once you've dug deep and you recognize what is driving your Delegate and Elevate activities, it's time to create your Personal Core Focus.

Just like a company's Core Focus, a Personal Core Focus has two hemispheres. Your purpose/cause/passion and your niche. Use your passions and strengths list to create a compelling purpose/cause or passion. Make your niche reflect your strengths. Your niche should be simple. Once you're happy with your results, update your Personal V/TO (see appendix).

Your finished Personal Core Focus should look something like this:

PERSONAL CORE FOCUS	PASSION: EMPOWERING INDIVIDUALS TO SEIZE THEIR POTENTIAL AND INSPIRING TRANSFORMATIVE ACTION FOR A FULFILLED FUTURE NICHE: SELLING

Your Personal Core Focus should be aligned with your seat on the Accountability Chart and the five roles you're accountable for. If they don't, you're probably in the wrong seat, and it's time to make a change.

STEP 5: DELEGATE, AUTOMATE, AND ELIMINATE

We can easily get bogged down by the activities outside our **Love/Great** quadrant. Doing activities outside our Personal Core Focus drains our energy and reduces our impact on the world. They can even affect our happiness and well-being.

You need to free yourself of these draining activities. They're holding you back. At least once per quarter, delegate, eliminate, or automate at least one activity from the bottom two quadrants. When you've eliminated everything in the bottom two, move to the top-right quadrant. That's when things start getting really good.

Remember that when you delegate, it's not about ego and status. You're elevating yourself to *your* Personal Core Focus. Don't do it by dragging someone outside of their Personal Core Focus. Make sure that what you're delegating is a great fit for who you're delegating to. If they can't do what you're delegating to them better than you ever could, chances are they aren't the right person.

STEP 6: CONTINUOUSLY UPDATE

We all learn and grow over time. Our interests and passions change over time. We're all a continuous work in progress and on a never-ending journey. Things that used to be in **Love/Great** will move to **Like/Good**, then at some point may drop down to **Don't Like/Good**, then finally **Don't Like/Not Good**. That's why we recommend going through this process at least once per year. If you want to really make an impact on your life and those around you, go through steps 1 through 5 every quarter or even more often if necessary.

By embracing your Personal Core Focus, you can unlock your full potential, drive personal and professional success, and create a lasting impact in your respective domains.

Another way to think of Personal Core Focus is:

SOMETHING YOU LOVE
+
SOMETHING YOU DO BETTER
THAN ANYONE ELSE IN THE WORLD

Let's break down this formula a little further.

Something You Love is a purpose and a passion that launches you out of your bed every morning, thrilled that you get to do what you do.

Something You Do Better Than Anyone Else in the World is what you're absolutely great at. It's your superpower, that ability that makes others marvel at how well you do it.

Give people this gift of a Personal Core Focus, and they'll love you forever, and they will not want to leave. Why? Because what people most want is the chance—that precious opportunity—to use their own unique talents and skills and experience in a way that contributes to the world in some special way. We'll return to this concept later in the book.

Why is unleashing human creative power so powerful and profitable? The simple answer is that it allows you to tap the ultimate resource: human ingenuity.

The economist Julian Simon says it well: "Ultimately, the ultimate resource is people—especially skilled, spirited, and hopeful young people endowed with liberty—who will exert their wills and imaginations for their own benefit and inevitably benefit the rest of us as well."

To create an enduring culture that wins in any market and in any environment, you must believe in and respect the unique contributions of each individual in your company. If you don't believe that each person on this planet is unique, you're unlikely to find this book helpful in your culture-building journey.

THIS IS NOT ABOUT RIDDING YOUR ORGANIZATION OF CONFLICT

We just painted a vision of a business culture using five keys to create a culture rooted in abundance and love. Some people take this idea and go one step further and assume we're talking about aiming for a workplace free from conflict. But that's taking the concept too far. Not only is that unrealistic, but also it would be unhealthy.

There are two types of conflict, productive conflict and unproductive conflict. Productive conflict is never personal—it's about striving for the Greater Good of the organization and the individual. Unproductive conflict is personal; it's about status and ego, pushing someone else down, making them wrong and offending them deeply.

Evaluating a work culture as "good" because of an absence of conflict stems from a mindset of fear and scarcity. In such an environment, conflict becomes an unwelcome guest, leading to hidden discussions and cautious behavior as employees strive to sidestep confronting interpersonal issues directly and transparently.

This is the kind of culture that leads to the secretive "meeting before the meeting" and the quiet "meeting after the meeting." Nothing good can come out of those conversations.

In a culture rooted in abundance and love, conflict can be dealt with productively, because there is trust. Problems are to be solved in the spirit of what works for the Greater Good. Problems are no longer bitter personal conflicts, but as our founder Gino Wickman says, "It's just an issue."

Conflict will never go away, and that should never be your goal. The aim should be to deal with problems and conflict productively and creatively. You cannot and will not get what you want from your business if you avoid conflict. Conflict and friction are the fuel for growth and progress, and should not be considered negative words.

We're realists. We've worked in the trenches as entrepreneurs and as coaches to entrepreneurs for too long to be anything else. So we acknowledge that it will never be perfect. We're all human, and we're going to do things like lose our patience at the wrong time or get snappish at the end of a long day.

There are also the hardships of personal lives that can impact anyone at work. In short, people issues can get particularly thorny. But if you realize the goal isn't complete utopia, you can accept that and then move in the right direction. You focus on making abundance and love the new normals at your business *most of the time.* That will have a tremendous impact on everyone's energy, motivation, and happiness.

If you could move the needle where 80 percent of the time your work culture was a place where everyone truly strived to make others feel valued and appreciated, the results would be transformative. We've seen it.

You'll never be a perfect leader, but if you're people-centric—if you genuinely put people first—you'll get it right more times than not. What all leaders have in common are followers. And people follow when they believe in you, when they trust you, and when they think you have their best interests at heart. If you don't, it will eventually catch up to you in one of two ways: your business will fail *or* you'll be "successful" but constantly miserable (and so will those around you).

Commit to making abundance and love the healthy soil that allows your intentional culture to grow, and the rewards will be huge. Once you make this commitment to heart-centered leadership and "putting the love in it," how do you go about structuring your team to make it happen? That's where we now turn.

REFLECTION QUESTIONS

1. Are there areas of your business that you're running from a place of scarcity and fear versus abundance and love?

2. Is your Personal Core Focus in alignment with the business Core Focus?
3. Is your Leadership Team 100 percent on the same page with *every word* of your vision?
4. Do you and all leaders and managers demonstrate Genuine Care and Concern for each of your people?
5. Are there areas where you're either not acknowledging, or holding back from leveraging, individual unique talents?

· · · · · · · · · · · · · · · · · · ·

"Changing the Leadership Team, changing the culture . . ."

Hazley Builders began implementing EOS in October 2020. It's a family business, and four brothers had just taken over the business from their father that fall.

All the brothers were on the Leadership Team, and they have since added two non-family members to the team, as well as one of their sisters.

The team has been creating significant transformations in their culture and business as a result of addressing people issues using EOS tools. They have been particularly good at being vulnerable, open, and honest. That allowed them to work through together that two of the brothers were in the wrong seat. Not only have the two brothers since moved into new roles creating new business units, the seats were backfilled with team members who "Get it, Want it, and have the Capacity for" those opportunities.

They took another big step just recently. After some simple questions about what was holding them back, they realized two other significant people moves had to be made if they were committed to an intentional culture. They took action, and it paid immediate dividends for creating a more open culture, and one more in line with their values.

They now have a much deeper understanding of the importance of their roles as leaders. They use EOS tools to set expectations and take action quickly on Right Person, Right Seat issues. They have been so inspired by the changes that they regularly share their insights with fellow entrepreneurs at their Remodelers Advantage industry roundtable meetings.

—Monica Justice, Certified EOS Implementer at EOS Worldwide

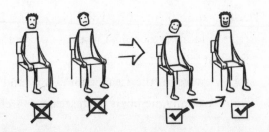

CHAPTER 3

. . . .

STRUCTURE FIRST

"VISION WITHOUT TRACTION IS HALLUCINATION."
 —GINO WICKMAN

After learning the basic concepts of intentional culture, many entrepreneurs start to get fired up. Great culture is inspiring, and the ideas start percolating.

This is the point where most entrepreneurs do what they love and are genuinely good at. They start moving rapidly in the direction of what intuitively feels like it should be the next step: to create a big vision around great values and huge, exciting goals. That's the fun stuff and it's completely understandable to want to go there first.

While that may feel like the most intuitive way forward, it's not the most effective. We will get to that soon, but not yet.

Companies first need to have habits and disciplines in place if they want lasting change. Structure is the necessary context for allowing a new culture to take root and grow. Without the right structure, the new culture will quickly return to the same old ruts. Problematic behaviors and chaotic team dynamics will return with a vengeance.

In EOS language, the changes you want to make will not happen without the right structure in place to get Traction.

The starting point for structure is to figure out what seats your organization needs on its Leadership Team, and then begin sorting through who are the right people to fill them. This is crucial because *everything* starts with the Leadership Team. As goes the Leadership Team, so goes the rest of the organization.

Your initial reaction to that might be *Wait, what? I already have a Leadership Team, and the slots are filled.* We'll get to that in a moment.

But first let's go deeper on why you start with your organization's structure before mapping out the vision of your business's culture and its values.

Think of it like this. Your current structure may be very much like a garden that needs attention. Your garden is weedy and has grown haphazardly. Some flowers may need to be pruned or replanted. Some will just need to be pulled out of the ground altogether. Others will need to be fertilized and nourished.

Also, maybe the garden needs an expansion to look like how you want it to eventually look. You can't expect to grow if you don't get in there with a shovel and expand its footprint and get the right seeds and nutrients. The right structure has to be in place before you can expect healthy and sustained growth.

As you think through your organization's structure, we recommend looking forward six to twelve months. Is your "garden plot" too small? Does your soil have the right nutrients? What is the right amount of sunlight and which seeds do you need to get the best results of the next six to twelve months?

It's the same way in your organization. You have to carefully think through the structure that will allow your culture to grow healthily. That begins with figuring out what the right seats are for your business. It's rare to find a business owner who launches a company asking what the right seats for their business are. And even if an entrepreneur did start with that question, the business grows and changes, and the original answers would soon be obsolete.

Without clarity around what you need now, your default position is that people are an interchangeable commodity. You end up seeing all your people as utility players, with abilities to do everything and move from one activity to another, people not being seen or positioned based on their Personal Core Focus. You end up with poorly defined positions (seats) and people who may not be up to filling them.

This becomes the perfect formula for a chaotic culture: unclear expectations plus the idea that people are interchangeable equals an entrepreneur who doesn't get what they want from their business. It's like watching a group of five-year-olds playing soccer. They're like bees swarming around the ball. There are no positions, no coordination. Some are picking flowers, and some are scoring for the other team. It's a chaotic mess.

Trying to build an intentional culture without first creating the right structure leads to similar chaos. To understand structure in the proper context, we need to first describe the EOS Process. After working with tens of thousands of companies, we find this process is the easiest and most reliable way to create a lasting impact in your business.

THE EOS PROCESS

Our proven process is designed to help you create the disciplines and habits necessary to execute every aspect of your vision. Whether you're self-implementing EOS or using a professionally trained EOS Implementer, we recommend you follow this process to get the most of the EOS Tools by getting your Leadership Team 100 percent on the same page right from the start.

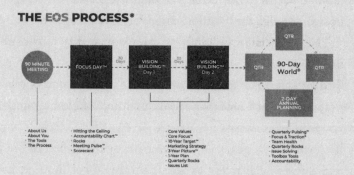

The first step in the EOS Process is the 90-Minute Meeting. During this meeting, we (or you) take your team through an overview of EOS. The point of the meeting is to gain buy-in from your Leadership Team that you want to go on this journey. This is the first time your team will see the People Component and the tools we use to achieve 80 percent-plus in all Six Key Components.

If you and your team decide that implementing EOS is for you, you schedule a **Focus Day.** The Focus Day is a full-day session, seven hours or so, that's dedicated to creating the context of Hitting the Ceiling. That inevitable feeling every company faces that makes it feel stuck and frustrated and what it takes to break through and get to the next level as a team.

We then create the **Accountability Chart** as a team. We focus just on the Leadership Team If we don't get that right, nothing else matters. Once we have the Accountability Chart right, we complete the other tools of Rocks, Meeting Pulse, and Scorecard. Each of these tools is defined in our other books in the *Traction Library*. (Visit eosworldwide.com/traction-library for more details.)

Next is **Vision Building** on days one and two. These days are dedicated to completing your Vision/Traction Organizer (V/TO) and getting your Leadership Team 100 percent on the same page with where you're going and how you'll get there.

From there, you'll meet with your team every quarter and once per year for two consecutive days creating a **90-Day World** to keep your team on the same page and executing well quarter after quarter.

Let's do a deeper dive on a crucial tool for building an intentional culture.

THE ACCOUNTABILITY CHART

The Accountability Chart (A/C) is an organizational chart on steroids. Creating one will be your guiding star for molding your organization into a structure that meets your business needs, and creates clear accountability for all the major functions of your business.

Detailed descriptions on this topic are covered in two other EOS books: chapter 4 of *Traction* and chapter 4 of *Rocket Fuel*. Both are great resources for understanding more about building out an A/C that supports you and your team getting everything you want from your business.

The aim of this chapter is to provide you with the basic, core steps of creating one and some additional guidelines and tips to help you get it right. Then we will tie it back to how it fits in with the goal of creating an intentional culture.

WHAT AN ACCOUNTABILITY CHART LOOKS LIKE

The following chart is an example, but you should know that each business's A/C is unique because no two businesses' needs are identical.

It starts by defining the Visionary and Integrator seats and who can best fulfill them. Every business has an owner, of course, but it's a mistake to think that the owner (or co-owners) automatically should be filling those seats.

It's true that the owner is often the Visionary, or sometimes the Integrator, or more rarely, both. But thinking of them as distinct seats with specific roles on the A/C is important. Every business needs the Right Person for these two crucial seats The Visionary and Integrator dynamic is such an essential combination that there

VISIONARY

- 20 Ideas
- Creativity/Problem Solving
- Big Relationships
- Culture
- R&D

INTEGRATOR

- LMA (Lead, Manage, Accountability)
- P & L/Business Plan
- Remove Obstacles & Barriers
- Special Projects

SALES/MKTG

- LMA
- Marketing
- Sales
- Hit Revenue/GM Goal
- Account Management

OPERATIONS

- LMA
- Customer Service
- Process Management
- Making the Product
- Providing the Service

FINANCE

- LMA
- Accounting
- Reporting
- IT
- HR/Admin

is an entire book devoted to the topic (*Rocket Fuel*), but here is a high-level summary:

VISIONARY (OFTEN THE OWNER, CO-OWNER, OR FOUNDER)

Common Roles
- Entrepreneurial "spark plug"
- Developer of new/big ideas/breakthroughs
- Big-problem solver
- Closing big deals
- Big relationships

Common Challenges
- Lack of clear direction/undercommunication
- Reluctance to let go
- Underdeveloped leaders and managers
- "Genius with a thousand helpers"
- Drive too intense for most people (burnout)

INTEGRATOR

Common Roles
- Leading, managing, accountability (LMA)
- Business plan execution/P&L results
- Resolving cross-functional issues
- Communication across the organization
- Remove obstacles and barriers

Common Challenges

- Job can be thankless
- Accusations of pessimism
- Being considered negative by others, as the "hole poker"
- Lack of recognition
- Being accused of moving too slowly

As we said, every business can be unique, but generally, it's fairly clear who the Visionary is. In most cases, they're the owner, CEO, and/or founder, or sometimes one-half of a co-owned business. One way to recognize a Visionary: they're the person coming up with tons of ideas, many of them bad or unrealistic. But they'll also find that one great idea a month or a quarter that will be brilliant and super impactful if executed.

While the right person for the Visionary seat is often clear, finding the right person for the Integrator seat is typically harder. It sometimes takes months or even a few tries to nail it. In our experience, the Integrator is usually the most challenging spot on the entire Accountability Chart to fill.

A good way to think about Integrators is that they need to be a *leader of leaders*. You're looking for someone with that X factor of leadership, the ability to engender trust and rally people around a common purpose. The Integrator is the steadying force that prevents Visionary whiplash (the tendency to try to implement a new trajectory every other day).

A COMMON TRAP WHEN FINDING YOUR INTEGRATOR

A mistake we've seen repeated many times is to leap immediately to a yes person as the Integrator. For every idea the Visionary proposes, they're ready to jump in and begin executing it.

It's natural to think that this could be the Integrator, because one of the things Integrators do is drive implementation of new initiatives.

But there's a serious flaw in this thinking. The Integrator isn't simply an effective foot soldier unquestionably carrying out the orders of a general. If someone is ready to say yes to everything (and too quickly), that's actually a sure sign that they're *not* an Integrator. A crucial part of this role is to be able to push back on the Visionary.

Left to his or her own devices, the Visionary will continue to chase too many different ideas, and all at once. The Integrator has to be someone who can pull the Visionary aside and talk sense about what can and cannot be reasonably accomplished.

Think of the Integrator as the filter of ideas. A yes person can't perform those roles.

If there's disagreement on a final decision among the Leadership Team, the Integrator needs to be completely and utterly trusted by the Visionary. A good Visionary recognizes that while they may be better at coming up with game-changing ideas, it's the Integrator who can be trusted to make a better decision on what's worth pursuing and how best to implement it.

A smart Visionary has enough self-awareness to understand that they can be a rash, quick starter and an extreme risk-taker. When the team is split and the decision isn't obvious, the Integrator is the better choice for making a final call. Visionaries have to trust enough to let go if this relationship is going to work.

The trust and confidence between a Visionary/Integrator (V/I) is everything. It can take some time to build, but it's a relationship worth mastering on both sides, because it will create a powerful dynamic of leadership for the company.

PLEASING VERSUS SERVING

There's a larger lesson here, one that needs to be understood through-out your entire culture. It comes down to this simple question: Do people in your organization look to be pleasers or servers?

When your organization has too many pleasers, the Greater Good we discussed in chapter 2 isn't served. People are stuck in fear mindsets ("If I please enough, I'll stay out of trouble and keep my job"), and scarcity mindsets ("Pleasing may not make things better, but at least, it protects the status quo.").

The Greater Good isn't about pleasing—it's about serving. The question is always, "How can I best *serve* the Greater Good of this business?"

So, while pleasing can *look like* serving, underneath, they're two opposite ideas. This is something that needs to be understood throughout your entire organization because wanting to please instead of looking to serve is such a common problem.

Let's return to the example of a Visionary and Integrator to bring this idea into clear focus. If the Visionary announces, "We're going to accomplish these twenty things this quarter," a pleaser says, "Yes, let's go get those twenty things done."

But a true Integrator will say, "We don't have the bandwidth to do these twenty things. Let's whittle it down to three things we can focus on and do really well." That's true serving.

Think of major professional sports teams that have an owner and a general manager. This is a recognition that while owners may set the tone for the entire organization, they're typically not going to be the best at guiding the day-to-day operations that best serve the team. That's why there's a general manager role. The idea behind having an Integrator is very similar.

This isn't just about healthy relationships; it's also a good business strategy. Strategy is a set of choices about what you'll do and what you won't do to create advantages over your competition and serve your customers well. More often than not, the better strategy is saying "no" to almost everything, and that's where an Integrator can really shine.

THE OTHER LEADERSHIP SEATS ON THE ACCOUNTABILITY CHART

While every business needs a Visionary and Integrator, after that there is never a one-size-fits-all solution for the rest of the seats on the A/C. Every business is unique.

However, one guideline to use as you create your chart is to think of the three major functions of any business: marketing and sales, operations, and finance and administration. Within those general categories, you need to figure out how to divide those functions into seats based on the needs of your business.

It could be as simple as one seat for finance and admin, one for sales and marketing, and one for operations. But it's rarely that cut-and-dried.

Maybe finance and admin needs multiple seats: HR, accounting, and IT. Another company may need to divide it up differently.

Let's look at a hypothetical: Say the company ABC Widgets & Stuff currently has a director of sales and marketing position. The company is doing a fantastic job with their marketing, attracting a healthy number of qualified leads. But sales aren't as robust as they should be, with below expected close rates. The questions the Leadership Team of this business need to be asking are as follows:

- Did we create sales and marketing as one position because a lot of other companies have a similar grouping and title?

- Would our business be better served with one seat for sales and one seat for marketing?

None of this is to recommend or prejudge the answer for any seat on the A/C in your specific business. Sometimes the answer is breaking a major function into multiple seat is best, and sometimes it isn't. But exploring it can lead to surprising and productive discussions.

CREATIVE WAYS TO NAVIGATE THIS PROCESS

Be prepared that things can get a little emotional as you create the A/C.

You can imagine that the director of sales and marketing at ABC Widgets & Stuff Company might be getting an uneasy feeling and a bit defensive as splitting her fiefdom into two seats is discussed. What will that mean for her? People get understandably anxious.

The key here is to not get too far ahead of the discussion. In this initial phase, you aren't worrying about current job titles or specific people.

It's a little like doing a puzzle. During the first part of the meeting, you're trying to get an idea of the picture on the box. What your company needs to accomplish is like the visual of the completed puzzle on the box.

Next, you dump all the pieces out. That's when you're transitioning in the meeting to creating the A/C (and yes, sometimes it can feel just as chaotic as a bunch of puzzle pieces spread out everywhere).

What strategy do most puzzle solvers employ first? They create the border of the puzzle. And that's exactly what you and your team are accomplishing. You're "fitting the edges together" by figuring out what leadership seats the company needs to best function.

Emotions begin to bubble up when a thought arises, *Do we have some extra pieces that belong to a different puzzle?* Put that aside for now and focus on what the right seats are for the good of the business.

A DARING THOUGHT

When helping teams through this process, some EOS Implementers have been known to announce to everyone at the meeting:

"Okay, you're all fired. You're done. You're outta here. There are no jobs here right now. Any possible leadership positions are floating somewhere in the ether above this conference table.

"But you're actually not just fired. You also are being temporarily promoted to the board of directors of this company. Now, as the board, we need to think about what seats we're going to create that best fit this organization."

What this does is it detaches the people in the room from their specific roles and gets them thinking more about the leadership structure the business truly needs.

Surprisingly often, "being fired" energizes people and opens up their creativity to think in new ways. They start exploring combining, separating, creating, and eliminating seats in a spirit of what would best serve the business—which is exactly what you want.

Obviously, whether you implement this specific technique in your own discussion is up to your good judgment based on your own personality and your team. But either way, it's a good thought experiment. The ability to think through the leadership needs of the business regardless of current slots is an essential step for creating a good Accountability Chart.

ACCOUNTABILITY CHART DOS AND DON'TS

DO *NOT* TRY TO PLAN TOO FAR OUT

Some Leadership Teams think they need to make an enduring work of art out of their Accountability Chart. Yes, it needs to be as good as you can make it now, but it isn't forever.

If you try to make it an everlasting masterpiece, you and your Leadership Team will feel that pressure. This freezes people up and makes change less appealing because it feels too permanent.

Your business is meant to grow and change, and you cannot and should not expect to create a permanent structure that will match the future. The culture of your business is a living thing, and your A/C needs to be a living, breathing document that grows with it.

A helpful analogy here can be to think of a child growing through adolescence. They grow naturally, but you usually know they're in a spurt because they experience growing pains. It's natural, but painful. When your business starts experiencing those cramps and pains of growth, an updated A/C will allow your business to hit the next growth ceiling. And then it will be time to do it again.

How far you plan out should be as unique as your business. We generally find that six to twelve months works for a lot of businesses—not too long, not too short. But some businesses have a specific challenge that may require a shorter cycle, while others are better equipped to do some longer-range planning into years.

How long an A/C can stay in place before it needs to change also has a lot to do with the company's growth rate. A business growing at a rapid pace of 20 percent can expect to modify their A/C in as little as ninety days. (Related to this, we'll discuss Hitting the Ceiling in a later chapter.)

ONE PERSON PER SEAT

Remember that the Accountability Chart is an org chart on steroids. This means there can be no fuzziness around who performs which roles within the organization. The intent is to inject maximum clarity and maximum accountability into the business.

That means you should never have more than one person in a seat It needs to be crystal clear who's responsible for that seat. If you have two people in one seat, accountability gets watered down, and things get muddled.

There can be situations where one person holds down multiple seats. In that scenario, the accountability for a particular function still clearly resides with just one person. As a general guideline, this shouldn't be the norm. Typically, it happens during times of high growth, transition after a person leaves, or other special circumstances.

LESS IS MORE

A common mistake is to create too many seats on the Leadership Team. With few exceptions, there should be between three and seven people at the helm of your organization. More seats tends to create less clarity and more working at cross purposes.

We have seen many examples where a Leadership Team gets cut in half (for example, from ten to five). In almost every case, productivity has gone up significantly.

This is known as the Ringelmann Effect. Productivity decreases as the team size increases. For example, studies have shown that a team of eight is less productive than a team of four in activities ranging from rope-pulling contests to solving business problems.

Think of it this way: if Disney, with hundreds of thousands of employees, can run on three major defined functions, then so can you.

COMPLETING THE CHART

Up to this point, we have been talking about the A/C mostly in terms of the Leadership Team. Once you have that completed (the border of the puzzle), you need to continue to fill in the picture by connecting everyone in your organization to it.

See the example on the following page.

FIVE ROLES PER SEAT

You'll notice on the chart that every seat lists five roles, because every seat in your organization should have five major roles, specifically and clearly defined.

Some other examples to help you customize your Accountability Chart for your unique organization:

For the Visionary, the roles might be research and development, big ideas, creative problem solving, big relationships, and closing big deals.

For a sales and marketing seat, the roles might be leadership, management, and accountability (LMA), hitting the revenue goal, the sales and marketing process, sales and marketing execution, and lead generation.

Each of the roles of each seat should be tied to a specific goal—something measurable. For example, in the sales and marketing process, that might mean measuring the number of phone calls made by the sales team that week. For the revenue goal, it would be whether they met the monthly quota. And so on.

Please also note that LMA is the first role for anyone who manages other people. We'll discuss LMA more in a later chapter, but for now just know this: in an intentional culture, developing, leading, and managing people is always going to be a priority.

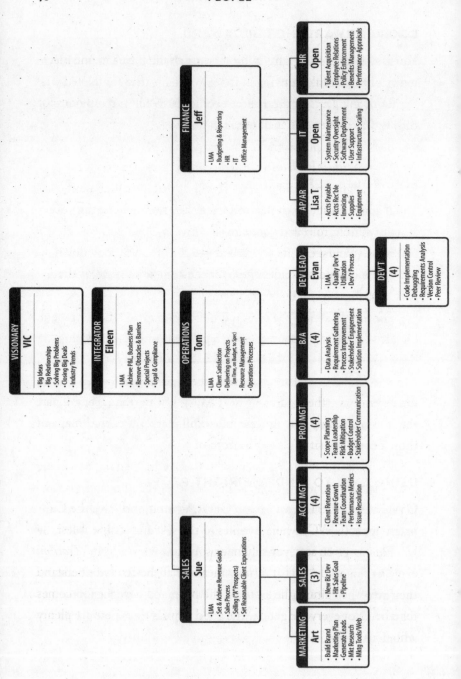

VISIONARY
VIC
- Big Ideas
- Big Relationships
- Solving Big Problems
- Closing Big Deals
- Industry Trends

INTEGRATOR
Eileen
- LMA
- Achieve P&L, Business Plan
- Remove Obstacles & Barriers
- Special Projects
- Legal & Compliance

SALES
Sue
- LMA
- Set & Achieve Revenue Goals
- Sales Process
- Selling ("A" Prospects)
- Set Reasonable Client Expectations

MARKETING
Art
- Build Brand
- Marketing Plan
- Generate Leads
- Mkt Research
- Mktg Tools/Web

SALES (3)
- New Biz Dev
- Hit Sales Goal
- Pipeline

OPERATIONS
Tom
- LMA
- Client Satisfaction
- Delivering on Projects (on Time, on Budget, to Spec)
- Resource Management
- Operations Processes

ACCT MGT (4)
- Client Retention
- Revenue Growth
- Team Coordination
- Performance Metrics
- Issue Resolution

PROJ MGT (4)
- Scope Planning
- Team Leadership
- Risk Mitigation
- Budget Control
- Stakeholder Communication

B/A (4)
- Data Analysis
- Requirement Gathering
- Process Improvement
- Stakeholder Engagement
- Solution Implementation

DEV LEAD
Evan
- LMA
- Quality Dev't
- Utilization
- Dev't Process

DEV T (4)
- Code Implementation
- Debugging
- Requirements Analysis
- Version Control
- Peer Review

FINANCE
Jeff
- LMA
- Budgeting & Reporting
- HR
- IT
- Office Management

AP/AR
Lisa T
- Accts Payable
- Accts Rec'ble
- Invoicing
- Supplies
- Equipment

IT
Open
- System Maintenance
- Security Oversight
- Software Deployment
- User Support
- Infrastructure Scaling

HR
Open
- Talent Acquisition
- Employee Relations
- Policy Enforcement
- Benefits Management
- Performance Appraisals

LOOK FORWARD, NOT BACKWARD

You may not get this right on the first try. Nailing this in one meeting is a big ask. Take a swing at it.

The book *Traction* gives three excellent guiding ground rules for this. From chapter 4 of the book:

1. You must look forward. You cannot look back or get caught up in the present. It will distort your judgment.
2. You must detach yourself from the existing business, your current role, and your ego.
3. You must elevate yourself above the business, look down on it, and make decisions for the long-term good of the company.

FILLING THE SEATS

Once you have the leadership seats on your Accountability Chart set, it's time to find the right people to fill them. Of course, many of those people are sitting right in front of you.

USING GWC TO FIND THE RIGHT PEOPLE

GWC stands for: Does a person Get it, Want it, and have the Capacity for it (GWC) when it comes to the seat and its five roles?

For any given seat, you first need someone who "gets it." *Traction* explains this well: "'Get it' simply means that they truly understand their role, the culture, the systems, the pace, and how the job comes together. Not everyone gets it. The good news is that there are plenty who do."

Next, do they want it? People will often say yes to a new seat without ever asking themselves, *But, okay, do I really want it?* We all know cases of promotions that people come to regret accepting. This leads backward to suck-it-up culture, where a person will just stay miserable or eventually leave.

You can see "want it" more in what people do than by what they say. Are they watching the clock, or do they come in with passion wanting to kill it every day?

Here is another telltale sign of a lack of "want it." Let's say the Leadership Team is discussing solving a problem in sales, and everyone is quite animated and intensely focused on coming up with a solution. The only person who doesn't seem to be contributing and passionate is the person in the sales leadership position seat. It happens more than you might think, and it's a surefire indicator that the person isn't right for the seat.

Get it and want it are both nonnegotiable to even be considered to fill a seat in the business. Then comes the final standard: do they have the capacity for it?

Do they have the skills, talent, and ability to fill the roles of the seat? Some seat require a heavier time commitment than others. Do they have that time? Do they have the knowledge to do the work? Do they have the mental, physical, and emotional ability to do the job well?

There can be a tiny bit of wiggle room here. Sometimes you could have someone who's currently a no on capacity for a particular seat but you believe they can get there. If you're going to take this risk, you have to be willing to invest the time and resources to get them there.

Example: A recent college graduate that you hired for a slot a little lower on the chart. They "get" the seat. They definitely "want" it. And you believe they can grow quickly into the capacity for the role.

Don't fall into the trap of doing this often. And don't use this as an excuse to put someone in a seat they don't have the capacity for just to avoid telling them no. It's also important to note that your organization has to have the resources and capacity to train and wait for the person to grow fully into the seat. If that isn't yet the case, don't try this.

THE GWC FLOW CHANNEL

As we described, people can be put in seats that they don't yet have the capacity for and if you can wait a few years until they gain the capacity, it may work. But how does GWC work over time? We have to recognize that people are in a constant state of change.

We've discovered that when someone truly GWCs their seat, they are in what Mihaly Csikszentmihalyi calls "flow." We've adapted this important concept to illustrate what GWC looks like over time and in changing contexts.

They may get bored as their skills grow and no longer want the seat they're in. You promote them, then the seat is too big and they're stressed out because they may no longer get it and have the capacity to do the job. However, what happens most often is the business grows and the demands and challenges of the seat grow and expectations rise. Remember: People don't rise to the occasion. We sink to the lowest level of our training and preparation.

The ideal GWC development can be illustrated on a simple two-axis graph, with the flow channel representing the sweet spot:

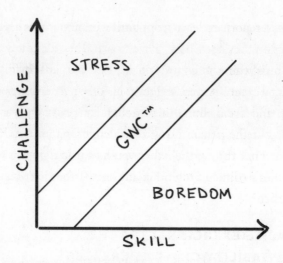

It's tempting to take a sink-or-swim or fake-it-until-you-make-it approach with your people. But without the proper support, people usually sink. They'll be filled with anxiety and stressed out. That doesn't mean you never want to stretch and challenge your people. It just means you need to find the right balance of challenge compared to their current skills.

Some of your team love big challenges way outside of their current skill sets, and some can only be stretched incrementally before shutting down. It's different for each person.

Make sure that you're always investing in your people with directed learning, one-on-one coaching and instructive experience. Directed learning is widely available in leadership and management training, and also on training for specific job skills. One-on-one coaching could be an outside executive coach or a mentor inside the organization. For example, Kelly Knight mentors a few team members on project management and other activities to help them level up in their roles at EOS Worldwide even though they don't report to her directly. Directed learning is instilling a process that leads to after-action reports to learn from both wins and losses and to adjust accordingly.

One final thing to consider for GWC is to ask it for each role of the seat Sometimes leaders get roles one, two, and three, but not roles four and five. Talking this through can lead to productive discussion about the person being considered for the seat. It also can make you think through whether you have the right structure. Are the five roles so difficult to find in any one person that you're looking for a unicorn?

A VALUABLE EXERCISE AFTER THE ACCOUNTABILITY CHART IS CREATED

After an A/C is created, the natural tendency will be to slot in the person who has the closest current job title to that seat. That will often be appropriate.

But here's a good exercise to make things honest, open, and vulnerable. Go around the room and have all the leaders do an on-the-spot performance appraisal of the person as a match for the seat. Use GWC as the guide.

Ask each of them, does this person get it? Does this person want it? And do they have the capacity for it? The answers often vary, but they will give you some insight. It also gets the person being appraised thinking, *Do I GWC this seat?* Keep in mind that you're looking for a solid yes-or-no answer on GWC. This isn't something where you settle for "maybe" or "kind of." There's no room for gray here.

Then do this with each of the other seats.

Does that sound like it will cause some upset? Sometimes it does. But again, you're trying to inject honesty and vulnerability so you can get to root issues. Remember: it takes courage to dare to

build an intentional culture. And that often means some (necessary) discomfort will be felt among everyone participating in the
exercise.

ARE THEY A LEADER?

As you fill seats, another rule should be this: to be on the Leadership
Team, the person needs to actually *be* a leader. It isn't unusual for
us to ask a business owner who's in charge of, say, sales, and get no
clear answer. In these cases, if there's a meeting of the Leadership
Team, the top salesperson gets invited. There may be good reasons
to at least consider that person for the leadership seat, but the top
salesperson isn't the same as the leader of your sales team.

We see this all the time in all different areas of a business:

"Who is in charge of finance?"

"Well, I have a bookkeeper. And I also have someone who does
payroll. And . . ."

That means there isn't one person in charge of that seat. This is
the kind of lack of clarity that you address with an A/C.

HAVING A TEAM OF GREAT PEOPLE
IS NOT A SOLUTION

Here's another belief to rid yourself of: that the solution is to create
a team of "great people." "Just tell me how to hire great people. I'll
hire the best, and then add them to the best that are already here.
Problem solved." We'll give you great hiring practices in chapter 8 to
help you find excellent people.

But if you think having great people is some kind of magic pill,
it isn't. It may be true that those people have a better chance of
working out, but the truth is that they have to be the right person
in *your* structure. They have to fit the specific seat in your unique

organization, not just be a "great person." They have to fit your business cycle (start-up, high-growth, mature, etc.). Again, it comes back to the A/C as the tool that gives structure for success.

VALIDATING THE ACCOUNTABILITY CHART

Traction also provides three questions to discuss with your Leadership Team to validate the Accountability Chart:

1. Is this the right structure to get us to the next level?
2. Are all of the Right People in the Right Seats?
3. Does everyone have enough time to do the job well?

COURAGE FOR THIS JOURNEY

Back in chapter 1, we shared that "courage matters" is one of the foundational concepts for building an intentional culture. Creating an Accountability Chart is the first test.

It isn't unusual if it sets you down the path to deal with dysfunction with one or more members of your Leadership Team.

Then, as you fill out the chart to include managers, more issues will likely surface. That will be a defining moment. It's your opportunity to seek one of two outcomes: squarely face people problems head-on or continue to gloss over them. You get to choose.

Because if this is your first pivot toward an intentional culture, it can be a shock to your company's system. We're trying to paint a realistic picture for you here. We certainly don't want to make this too bleak. There is a big reward for going on the journey, but we would be misleading you if we said the road always feels smooth.

Let's return to the idea mentioned earlier about everyone having a Personal Core Focus that's unique to them. For everyone, there's a puzzle where they're the right piece.

This means that for everyone currently in your organization, there is one of four possibilities:

- They're right for your organization but in the wrong place at the moment (Right Person, Wrong Seat).

- They're competent or even excellent in their current seat, but their happiness and values would better match a different company (Wrong Person, Right Seat).

- They're the wrong fit for your organization, and they're in the wrong seat (Wrong Person, Wrong Seat).

- They belong in your organization, and they're already in the exact right place (Right Person, Right Seat).

It would be wonderful if most of the time the last one just happened naturally, but that isn't always the way it goes. This goes back to the nonintentional (haphazard) way most teams grow. Now that it's time to transition to an intentional culture, you need to dig deep and find the courage to say, "I want all of the people to find the place where they can best use their God-given talents."

In short, people don't just have precious gifts; they *are* precious gifts. They're doing themselves and everyone around them a disservice if they aren't in the right seat or the right organization to pursue that.

Some entrepreneurs are electrified by this vision right away and use it as fuel to push through the changes that will take their organizations to new heights. Others take more time to see it and fully put their faith in it.

If you act with authenticity, trust, and for the Greater Good, you'll transform your organization and change lives. To fully create those transformations, however, you need some solid values to build upon.

IT ALL STARTS WITH THE LEADERSHIP TEAM

In the journey of building an intentional culture, the Leadership Team plays a pivotal role. The leadership team is the nucleus of your organization, setting the tone for the entire company. They're the ones who embody the Core Values, drive the vision, and set the pace for the rest of the team.

In the EOS Model, the Leadership Team is the driving force behind the Six Key Components: Vision, People, Data, Issues, Process, and Traction. They're the ones who ensure that these components are strengthened and aligned, leading to a healthy and productive organization.

The Leadership Team isn't just about having people in positions of authority. It's about having the right people in those positions. The right people are those who understand their roles and have the capacity to perform their duties effectively. They're not just leaders in title, but in action and influence.

Gino Wickman defines strong Leadership Team by these seven criteria:

1. You have rock stars in every seat on the Leadership Team, with each member embodying the company's Core Values and having total confidence and trust in their fellow team members.
2. They're 100 percent on the same page with the vision and plan, agreeing on every word in the Vision/Traction Organizer™ (V/TO).
3. They speak one language, agreeing to use one common language throughout the organization and run on one operating system.
4. They're open and honest, comfortable with conflict and able to call out every issue and discuss them until they're resolved.
5. They're fanatical about resolution, solving five to fifteen issues every week in their weekly meeting and thirty per quarter in their quarterly planning sessions.
6. They treat each other as equals, ignoring hierarchy and ensuring an equal exchange of dialogue.
7. They possess the secret sauce: they love each other. They look forward to meeting together, and those meetings are passionate, intense, exhausting, fun, and never boring.

The leadership team's effectiveness isn't just measured by the company's financial success, but also by the health of its culture. A strong Leadership Team cultivates an environment where everyone feels valued, appreciated, and connected to the purpose of the business. They foster a culture of accountability, where everyone takes ownership of their roles.

However, building such a Leadership Team isn't an overnight process. It requires intentionality, courage, and commitment. It involves making tough decisions, having difficult conversations, and sometimes, letting go of people who aren't the right fit. It's about prioritizing the long-term health of the organization over short-term gains.

In the end, you cannot succeed without a great Leadership Team. A strong, aligned Leadership Team is the cornerstone of a thriving, intentional culture. They're the ones who will guide your organization toward success, making it a place where people are excited to come to work, and where they feel they're part of something bigger than themselves.

Remember: as a leader, you set the tone. Your actions, decisions, and behaviors have a ripple effect throughout the entire company. Stay focused on building a Leadership Team that embodies your Core Values, drives your vision, and fosters a culture of accountability and excellence. Because when you get the Leadership Team right, everything else falls into place.

REFLECTION QUESTIONS

1. Do you have an Accountability Chart in place, with clear seatsand roles, that's forward-looking six to twelve months out?
2. Can you answer yes to the three questions to validate your Accountability Chart?
3. Do you have a strong Visionary and Integrator relationship in place?
4. Does your Leadership Team possess the seven attributes of a great Leadership Team?
5. Do you have any people outside of the GWC Flow Channel experiencing boredom or stress?

• • • • • • • • • • • • • • • • • •

"I can't imagine how long we would have continued on with the wrong structure."

I worked for my family's business, a human services organization in the Twin Cities, for over sixteen years. About ten years into my time there, we began working with Expert EOS Implementer Sue Hawkes. At the time of implementation, our Leadership Team was pretty large, consisting of me (in a hodgepodge admin role), my dad (CEO), mom (HR), sister (president), husband (property manager), and two other close friends (both in business development).

Our family dynamics as well as the somewhat haphazard development of our roles and organizational structure made the Accountability Chart exercise very interesting. The words were said to us:

"You're all fired from your jobs. We're now going to put together a structure that serves the Greater Good of your company." As we began piecing together what the Accountability Chart should look like, the size of the Leadership Team, at least as represented on the whiteboard, began to shrink. My stomach began to turn as I realized what that meant.

The first point of major discomfort was when my husband's seat property manager, was no longer on the Leadership Team level. Tension began to grow in the room. Then, it was decided that we don't need two business development seats on the team. More tension. And last, there were no hodgepodge admin seats on the Leadership Team. The room was thick with anticipation.

Next, it was time to put our names into the new Accountability Chart we just created. We began with the HR seat and the question was asked, "Who wants this seat" To everyone's surprise two hands went up: my mom's and mine. My motivation was not to do whatever possible to remain on the Leadership Team. I actually really wanted the HR role. I was ready for growth and a challenge. It excited me.

My mom has always been my best friend, and then suddenly my mom and I are in the midst of a bake-off for who is the best fit for the role, and I won. I was excited and mortified at the same time. Next on the agenda, the business development seat. Another upset happened when we collectively decided the younger, greener guy was chosen for the role on the Leadership Team over the older, more seasoned guy because of his natural leadership abilities.

And last, it was decided my husband belonged squarely in the property management role and would no longer be a part of the Leadership Team. By the end of the day, we all still had jobs, but we had cut my mom, husband, and our good friend from the Leadership Team This had the potential to be explosive and incredibly destructive to our relationships. Feelings were a bit hurt, but everyone was genuinely on board with the results because as we walked through the exercise, the truth was revealed that my mom no longer wanted to carry the burden of our HR department, my husband was not truly interested in leading at the Leadership Team level, and our good friend did not have the natural skills required to lead in business development.

In the end, we were all happy with the result because these were truly the right decisions for the good of the company. This new structure made us much more effective and was a big turning point in our organization. Yet, without our EOS Implementer leading this discussion, we never would have been able to have these discussions or come to these conclusions. I can't imagine how long we would have continued on with the wrong structure, likely enduring much pain until we were willing to have the hard conversations.

—Ali Wendt, director of employee services for Supportive Living Solutions(Ali has since joined EOS as a Professional EOS Implementer.)

CHAPTER 4

. . . .

GETTING TO THE CORE OF YOUR CULTURE

"YOUR BELIEFS BECOME YOUR THOUGHTS,
YOUR THOUGHTS BECOME YOUR WORDS,
YOUR WORDS BECOME YOUR ACTIONS,
YOUR ACTIONS BECOME YOUR HABITS,
YOUR HABITS BECOME YOUR VALUES,
YOUR VALUES BECOME YOUR DESTINY."
—MAHATMA GANDHI

If you don't have a clear set of Core Values that you can state with complete confidence and clarity, you have zero chance of building an intentional culture.

This may sound a bit over-the-top. Aren't Core Values a "nice-to-have," something to hang on the walls to remind team members to act with integrity and to provide good service? You can post them on the website, too, to tell customers something about your company. It's good marketing, if nothing else. Besides, there are probably more pressing problems to solve. You can always get to Core Values later.

We understand why many business owners feel this way about Core Values. Unfortunately, many online articles and standard business advice have made the phrase "Core Values" a meaningless "feels-good" thing. Core Values in this sense reeks of posters in the lunch room that no one cares about.

They're also sometimes seen as a marketing ploy, something to brag about on your website or to print on coffee mugs you hand out to your customers.

This is unfortunate, because a lackluster mindset toward Core Values is actually what holds businesses back. An organization gets better at problem solving—and prevents many problems from ever happening—when they build an intentional culture around a set of clear Core Values.

WHY CORE VALUES MATTER FOR INTENTIONAL CULTURE

In a way, you could say Core Values put the intention in intentional culture. Once they're clearly articulated, you'll hire and fire based on them. You'll recognize, reward, and review using them as the standard. When you do it right, everyone in your company will use the values as a guide to reinforce the rules of engagement and cultivate the type of culture that attracts the right people for your organization.

At EOS, we often help business owners visualize the goal of the People Component as "getting all your arrows pointed in the same direction." Everyone in your business has a basic orientation toward how they go about what they do and what values they exhibit at work.

When we first encounter a business, it's common to find people pointed every which way, and the result is lots of human energy wasted and unproductive conflict. In the absence of clearly defined values, people will naturally work in whatever direction feels right to them, or often just do the equivalent of aimlessly wandering. Recall these diagrams from chapter 1:

THE HUMAN ENERGY MODEL

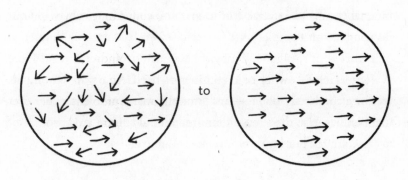

Discerning and defining Core Values is a crucial part of getting the human energy in your business pointed in the same direction. It's a way to clearly identify which way the arrows are supposed to be pointing. And once you have that standard in place, the arrows pointing in other directions stand out. Then as your Core Values take root, the folks who don't fit begin to leave, which is a good thing for building an intentional culture.

Then if hiring is done the right way (see chapter 8), a critical mass develops. More and more arrows are pointed the same way, and the few who don't stick out more and more.

To be sure, getting a fully aligned Human Energy Model working at a maximum will require alignment across all the key EOS tools. But Core Values are an absolutely vital ingredient.

In short, Core Values reveal the fundamental standards for being and acting within your business. You use them to relentlessly pursue building your culture around those who share and are inspired by those values.

Okay, how do you go about discovering your Core Values?

DISCOVERING YOUR CORE VALUES

Here is the EOS exercise for discovering your Core Values. (For a deeper dive on completing this exercise, we recommend chapter 3 of *Traction*):

If you're the owner or a member of the Leadership Team and you haven't already done so, we strongly urge you to discover your Core Values. Use the simple four-step method below to do so.

Two quick but important notes before you dive in:

- Be sure to do this as a team; if someone tries to do this alone, the results are likely to be off-base.
- It should also be noted that you aren't voting on Core Values, with the most popular answers winning. And you aren't making them up based on what you want to be. You're discovering and discerning them. We'll develop this idea more below, but it's good to understand this from the very start.

Exercise

1. Think about three people in your organization today who you admire and wish you could clone. You know who they

are. They're the ones you wish others would emulate. Write down their names.

2. Now, think about the qualities, attributes, and characteristics that make these people such valuable assets. If you had a hundred people like them, you could dominate your industry. Think about what makes them who they are, the things you can't teach that are inherent.

3. Write all these characteristics on a sheet of paper. When you've finished your list, carefully examine what you've written. Your Core Values lie somewhere within these characteristics. Choose the best three to seven (less is more) that clearly articulate what you value.

4. Next, write each of them as short and sweet statements or phrases that would require very little elaboration or definition. Often, the right word or phrase resonates quickly with the right people and is more memorable. As an example, one of our clients uses the word *foxhole* to express a Core Value of digging in and working well together. Another client uses *funergetic* to express a Core Value of having fun and bringing positive energy to work.

WHAT CORE VALUE DISCUSSIONS ARE LIKE

You may find your team gets inspired during a Core Values discussion. Ideas creatively fly around fast and loose, are debated, and refined.

Other teams don't warm to the discussion as fast. That typically happens for one of two reasons. One reason is that the organization leaders believe they already have Core Values. They might, but in most cases, they're so weakly defined and so universally ignored in day-to-day business as to be worthless.

The other reason is that some Leadership Teams are a little more traditional in their approach. These teams use a fact-finding, analytical approach to solving problems, which is great for some issues. But discovering and articulating Core Values is a tremendously personal and heartfelt mission for a company. It needs to be tackled with more than dry analysis.

YOU CAN'T DO EITHER OF THESE IF YOU WANT THIS TO WORK

Sometimes a Leadership Team suggests delegating Core Values creation to their marketing department. This shows a fundamental misunderstanding of what this is really about.

If you think of them as something to polish up your reputation for the outside world, you're defining yourself externally. Core Values are the internal principles for action and behavior. Your customers will of course notice the impact of your Core Values, but it starts from an internal place of authenticity.

Delegating this to marketing will not work. We also occasionally hear the suggestion to bring in consultants or outsource it in some other way. The thought being that, once the Core Values are created, the Leadership Team can just step in and approve them.

Not to go on the attack here, but you want to outsource figuring out who you are? We hope it's obvious that won't work either.

Also, as we mentioned above, this isn't something to put up for a vote to the entire company. The Leadership Team needs to lead here and do the hard work of discerning the Core Values.

YOU DECIDE WHAT IS APPROPRIATE

Here are some rules for the wording of your Core Values:

- No profanity.
- Don't word them as a negative (as in "We *never*…" or "Don't…").
- Keep them general enough that no one could possibly be offended.

Okay, actually, none of these are rules. As soon as you let others put restrictions on how you express your Core Values, you've lost the point of Core Values.

One of our clients has as a Core Value that they express as "Fun as F—" (although they spell it out). That may not match your company. You may even hate it. But it suits them. And it tells people who may be applying to the organization: "If that idea doesn't fit you, or that way of saying it doesn't fit you, we're not a match."

One of our Core Values at EOS Worldwide is "Grow or Die." It's the simplest way we've found to help our team, and those we recruit, understand that this value represents how we're much more uncomfortable with the status quo than the prospect of change. We strive to take something that's good and make it superb. That's "Grow or Die."

Some people no doubt would be uncomfortable with the use of the word *die* in this Core Value. We understand, and that's the number one reason why you must define Core Values in the language that best fits your company—not the business down the street or your competitor. It tells people who you are and gives them a way to judge whether they're a perfect match. Or not.

THREE CORE VALUES TRAPS

There are three Core Values traps you want to avoid, as described by Patrick Lencioni in his *Harvard Business Review* article "Make

Your Values Mean Something." He articulates the traps beautifully as Permission to Play, Accidental, and Aspirational.

One of the most common Core Value traps is naming a value that simply grants you Permission to Play, as in, without it, you could not even "play" in your industry.

For example, let's say you're in an industry that requires extremely high safety standards and that this is monitored closely throughout the industry. If you propose a Core Value that states, "Safety is always a top priority," not only is that bland language, but it also doesn't differentiate you in any way from your competitors. If everyone emphasizes safety because otherwise they'd be out of business, that isn't a differentiating Core Value.

Another example of a Permission to Play trap is to pick some generalized virtue that no one could be against, as in, "One of our Core Values is integrity." It's good to have integrity, of course, and hopefully, you and your team have lots of it. But without further exploration, it isn't clear and specific enough. But things get more interesting if you start asking more questions.

- When you think of the word *integrity*, what does it mean to you?
- How do those meanings get expressed specifically here at work?

This allows you and your team to drill down and collect detailed examples. If the specific examples actually sound kind of vague and uninspiring, steer away from it as a Core Value.

If on the other hand, people get fired up, begin gushing out examples one on top of the other, you've found something.

The second Core Values trap is an Accidental value. These are values that exist within the organization, but they don't exist with leadership intent. For example, you may be an engineering firm and think that you have a Core Value of "Attention to Detail." Well, your engineers building bridges better pay attention to detail because that's what they were trained to do. But your salesperson doesn't need to pay attention to the details very often, or it might bog them down trying to grow revenues.

The third Core Values trap is Aspirational. These are values that you wish you had, but if you're being honest with yourself, you don't. These usually come about when the Leadership Team is trying to fix behaviors they see in their people that they don't like. But, again, if they were being honest with themselves they don't display those values either. We will use the same example of "Attention to Detail." Let's say your team keeps making errors and mistakes in the billing process and other areas of the business. The team wants the errors to stop, so they're tempted to create a Core Value of "Attention to Detail" when in reality they have a different type of people issue.

While creating your Core Values, make sure to avoid these pitfalls and make your values authentic.

GUIDELINES FOR THE PROCESS

During the first Core Values meeting, you're looking to get things about 80 percent of the way there. They don't have to be perfectly worded yet, and you don't have to be completely certain you've nailed all the right ones.

Then give yourself and the Leadership Team homework. Take the Core Values you've created and live them out for a month.

Notice them in others (or sometimes not) on the team. Observe examples of them in interactions with clients, vendors, and other outside partners.

Do they fit? Are they revealing how you're different? Are they speaking to what matters most to the organization? Reconvene in thirty days and discuss. If you discover that you have them right, do some final wordsmithing to make them short, clear, and powerful.

Be ruthless in editing, and remember that when it comes to the number of words, less is more. Your team members need to be capable of reciting, remembering and acting on these every day. Some "nice" teams avoid ruthless editing and then water down values to the point of meaninglessness.

Limit your total number of Core Values to somewhere between three and seven. This is definitely an area where less is more. These are Core Values that you expect your entire team to memorize, live by, call out, and so on. Creating fifteen Core Values is just not going to be realistic, memorable, or easy for your team to state simply and clearly.

You'll also be using these values in the hiring process, and if you have too many, your prospective candidates are going to be confused. They're going to question who you really are and unable to assess if they fit them all.

Once you've finalized your Core Values, it's time to deliver them in a speech. The purpose of the Core Values Speech is to communicate these values to your entire company. *Traction* describes this well: "It's time to create your Core Values Speech. People won't necessarily understand what you mean if you merely state each Core Value. That's why each one needs to be backed up with stories, analogies, and creative illustrations to drive home its importance."

Let's end with a few real-life examples of Core Values from some of our clients:

- Caring for Individuals and Families
- Always Learning and Progressing Together
- Trailblazing
- Producing Trust and Value
- Bring It—Dependable. Energetic. Confident.
- Own It—Willing. Committed. Accountable.
- Love It—Team Work. Learning. Respect.
- Do It—Proactive. Great Work.
- People First
- Passionate Pursuit of Fulfillment
- Pride in Ownership
- Perpetual Innovation
- Hustle and Amp
- One Team
- Entrepreneurial Mindset
- Relationships First
- Fun as F—
- Know It—Your Role, Customers, Number(s); Always Learning
- Live It—Where You're Supposed to Be; What You Say You'll Do
- Love It—Be Passionate; Be Team; Be Family; Have Fun!

Time for the next challenge. Once you have your Core Values defined and announced, how do you make sure they stick?

TIPS FOR A GREAT CORE VALUES SPEECH

You should have your own unique style to deliver your Core Values Speech. However, we've found there are some best practices that generally work best.

For example, at EOS we have created a simple format to build a Core Values Speech. These are key "talking points," and then our leaders use this to personalize their speech:

Be Humbly Confident
- No arrogance
- Know your stuff
- Be vulnerable—you're not perfect

Grow or Die
- More uncomfortable with the status quo than the prospect of change
- "Maximizer" (taking something strong to something superb)

Help First
- Must provide value before receiving anything
- You get out of life what you want if you help enough people get what they want
- Genuinely get a high from helping people

Do the Right Thing
- Enter the danger
- No amount of money is worth betraying a trust
- If Mom were watching...

Do What You Say
- Show up on time
- Fully deliver
- It's okay to say no
- Take the responsibility—blame no one
- Finish what you start

We then follow up these key points with tips for delivering it effectively:

When you deliver your speech, here are the keys to embedding your values and creating a common understanding throughout your organization.

- Personalize it: Share personal stories or experiences that demonstrate each Core Value. This makes the values more relatable and memorable.
- Consistency is key: Deliver your Core Values Speech the same way each time. Every leader should be able to deliver the speech with absolute consistency. Create a script if necessary.
- Frequency is a must: People need to hear it seven times to hear it for the first time. Your people should hear your Core Values Speech during the interview process and at least once per quarter from their leaders. Include the Core Values Speech in your Quarterly State of the Company.

Here's an example script we use at EOS Worldwide for our Core Values Speech.

Starting with our Core Values. Just as you teach every one of your clients, this is how we hire, fire, review, reward, and recognize each of our employees here at EOS Worldwide, and it's the standard for being a member of this community.

- *Be Humbly Confident*
- *Grow or Die*
- *Help First*
- *Do the Right Thing*
- *Do What You Say*

We are going to do a little checkup from the neck up. You don't need to draw out the People Analyzer (see page 134 and the Appendix)—just do it mentally and do some self-reflection.

Remember plus (+) is most of the time you share this Core Value; plus/minus (+/-) is sometimes you do, sometimes you don't; minus (-) is most of the time you do not.

Here at EOS Worldwide we are **Humbly Confident***.*

We abhor arrogance and yet we know our stuff.

We are vulnerable—we know we aren't perfect. We make mistakes.

We **Grow or Die***.*

We are more uncomfortable with the status quo than the prospect of change.

We are maximizers—we take something from strong to something superb.

We are on the path to mastery. There is no destination. We are just looking to get better each and every day.

*We **help first**.*

    We believe that we must provide value before we receive anything.

    This is about abundance—having the confidence to give it away and create value, knowing that there's more than enough to go around.

    We believe that you get out of life what you want if you help enough people get what they want.

    But that's not why we help—we help because we genuinely get a high out of helping people.

*We do **the right thing**.*

    We enter the danger. Some of you might be holding back with clients because you're afraid of ticking them off and losing them. That's scarcity thinking. That's not who we are. We believe in abundance and that gives us the confidence to have hard conversations and enter the danger without fear of losing them. We approach our clients with abundance and love versus scarcity and fear.

    We believe that there's no amount of money worth betraying a trust. That's why we don't pay referral fees to connectors or partners. You must always have the best interest of your clients in mind and not make decisions based on money.

    We are always asking if Mom was watching.

*We **do what we say**.*

    We show up on time.

    We fully deliver.

    We believe it's okay to say no.

    We take responsibility and blame no one.

We always finish what we start.

These are our Core Values. If you don't believe in these Core Values, you simply can't be here.

Please leave if you don't. Go find the organization that does fit your Core Values. You only have one life to live—you don't need to spend it with us.

I want to make sure that you love this place. That you love these people, you love your clients, and you love your work.

A powerful Core Values Speech is worth taking the time to craft, because it's a fundamental ingredient to embed Core Values deep in your company's culture.

REFLECTION QUESTIONS

1. Have you established your Core Values in your business?
2. Do any of your Core Values fall into one of the Core Value traps?
3. Do you have a Core Values Speech that you share consistently with your team each quarter?
4. Is the language of your Core Values embedded into your common language?
5. When you reflect on your Core Values, are there any people issues or people you're uncertain about?

• • • • • • • • • • • • • • • • • • •

"For anyone who doubts the power of Core Values . . ."

Many business leaders will roll their eyes at the concept of Core Values. And they're right to do so, as countless organizations have announced their fancy vision-and-mission statement and new values, only to immediately relegate them to an obscure spot on their website and never speak of them again. Or worse, state the organization's Core Values but then fail to create a culture of leadership that lives up to it.

It's no wonder that many are cynical about Core Values and see them as a fluffy, meaningless wastes of time and money that aren't relevant to real business and leadership.

But there's an organization that proves this wrong and demonstrates that Core Values need to be a critical component to creating a world-class organization. You just have to do it the right way.

As a former drill sergeant in the US Army, I've seen it firsthand. The army is nearly 250 years old, has over one million soldiers, and is the greatest fighting force the world has ever seen.

From day one of boot camp, soldiers are taught the history of the army, its Core Values, and the soldier's creed. They're expected to memorize them, live them, and enforce it with their team. Drill sergeants speak of the Core Values routinely to develop the culture of the team and set an example of what being a US Army soldier looks like.

The army's Core Values are Loyalty, Duty, Respect, Selfless Service, Honor, Integrity, and Personal Courage, forming a nice acronym: LDRSHIP.

These values shape the army's onboarding experience (boot camp) in every way and are infused into physical training, personal development, marksmanship, drill, and ceremonial events. They're also an essential part of every major milestone of a soldier's leadership development throughout their career.

For every promotion, award, and quarterly and annual evaluations, the values serve as an anchor for those conversations and decisions. Violations of the army's Core Values aren't tolerated at any level, and that's what makes the culture of the army so strong. This shared set of values is what allows teams and leaders from anywhere in the army to come together easily and work as a team regardless of geography, functional area, or position. It's also what shapes soldiers' actions and leadership in times of incredible stress and fear, such as combat.

For anyone who doubts the power of Core Values, you need to commit to them and create a culture that leads your team to live them out. Only then can you experience their power.

**—Rodney Mueller, former Army drill sergeant
and current Professional EOS Implementer**

CHAPTER 5

. . . .

CHOOSING TO TRULY TRANSFORM

"IT ALWAYS SEEMS IMPOSSIBLE UNTIL IT'S DONE."
—NELSON MANDELA

Right after you deliver your Core Values Speech, you're at an absolutely crucial fork in the path. Will you take the road less traveled?

You've likely been down the path of new initiatives with your team before. For many businesses, new plans are announced with great fanfare. It's a ball of fire and motivation at first, and then it often flames out once the early excitement wears off.

Then it's on to reading another business book or attending another mastermind, with another new idea, another initiative, and so on. Cue the hamster wheel.

Imagine what new announcements must look like to managers and entry-level employees. They may have a case of organizational whiplash from trying to keep up with all the twists and turns of each new idea.

From their perspective, this could have a "here-we-go-again" feel to it, and you'll have to work through that jadedness and prove to them that this is real change that the entire Leadership Team believes in and is 100 percent behind.

Even if you've not been guilty of too many past initiatives with too little results, this is still introducing something that's new and impactful, and that means a significant amount of reinforcement is needed before you expect anything to start sticking.

So, how do you make this a reality?

IMPLANT CORE VALUES DEEP INTO YOUR COMPANY'S HEART

It's as simple and as hard as this: make the language of your Core Values the foundation of how your company thinks and communicates. It should be observable in actions, behaviors, and words throughout the entire organization. Your Core Values need to form the heart of your culture and become the natural lens through which your entire team views engaging with one another, your clients, your partners, collaborators, and all other stakeholders.

The only way this can happen is to get the language of your Core Values deeply embedded into the communication of your team on a day-to-day basis.

If a person hears their team leader use some Core Values language two or three times, that will have little impact. But the seventh time? The fifteenth time? The hundredth time? Okay, now they're getting it. This time the commitment is real, trusted, and consistently observed.

SEE IT AND PRAISE IT

The entire Leadership Team needs to consciously look for examples of Core Values in action, and then praise those that have exhibited behaviors, words, and actions that demonstrate a specific company Core Value. Sometimes that's best done privately, one-on-one, and other times it may be publicly offered. You'll want to get curious about how that works best for different individuals and teams, rather than to assume it's a one-size-fits-all approach.

At first, watching for Core Values in action will be done very deliberately and consciously; but done enough times, and using consistent Core Values language, it becomes second nature.

Nothing will make this take hold faster than an intentional effort on the part of your entire Leadership Team. Notice a few things about the psychology of this method.

- First, actions called out on the spot allow for individuals and/or teams to immediately experience that the Leadership Team is seriously invested in Core Values being critical to the development of culture.
- Second, praise is often done in public. This impacts everyone within earshot. The person who receives it feels great, but just as important, others begin to strive for recognition for their efforts too. You'll make the heroes of your company those folks who are walking embodiments of your Core Values.
- And lastly, praise happens in the language of the Core Values. This normalizes and naturalizes these values, injecting them into the lifeblood of your company. The team as a whole begins to give others recognition for Core Values seen and observed.

Let's randomly select a few Core Value examples from the end of the last chapter and show how this can work: One Team, Perpetual Innovation, People First.

Someone volunteers to stay late so a coworker can get to their kid's school function on time. Their team leader says, "Wow, that's really exhibiting 'One Team' in caring for members of our team and making a positive impact in their family's life."

A manager suggests a tweak to the manufacturing process that will save thousands of dollars a year. Her boss makes a point of praising her in front of the entire company during a State of the Company presentation. "Sandy exemplified 'Perpetual Innovation'—in improving and strengthening our Process component. Way to be a creative problem solver, Sandy."

The Visionary overhears a customer-service rep bend over backward resolving a customer issue. When the call is over, the Visionary walks over. "Now that's exactly what we mean by 'People First.' You showed Genuine Care and Concern in a situation where the customer was particularly agitated and difficult. Well done."

It's crucial to understand that a standard shout-out for good work isn't enough. You want to be as specific as possible about the concrete **actions**, **behavior**, or **words** that exemplified a particular Core Value, and then tie it directly to the value. A vague call out isn't enough to make change happen.

Actions, *behavior*, and *words* are bolded in the previous paragraph for a reason. Ultimately, Core Values only make a difference if they manifest themselves in actions, behavior, and words. Core Values are deeply held beliefs, yes. But they only have real-world impact when demonstrated. Train yourself and your team to see and praise those actions, behaviors, and words.

THE CASCADING EFFECT

One of the most powerful aspects of this is the compounding effect this will have as Core Values language cascades throughout the organization.

This reminds us of a small but telling incident witnessed in a business we were helping. This company had a Core Value of providing "Outrageous Service." The value applied to both external customers and the service they provided to each other internally.

Working on the assembly line, one guy noticed something great one of his coworkers had done for another. Perhaps in the past, he would have said, "Hey, that was a cool thing you did," and that would have been that. Or maybe he wouldn't be on the lookout for something like it at all.

Instead, he called out loudly, "That was outrageous!" He now had the Core Values language for it and could see it in those terms. And by saying it out loud, he reinforced for himself and his coworkers that that was why they were there every day: to provide Outrageous Service.

This is how Core Values become more and more contagious, and that's when real change happens. When you witness something similar in your own organization for the first time, step back and smile. You know then that intentional culture is beginning to grab your company's heart.

IGNITING MANAGERS CAN BE A TIPPING POINT

In our observations working with businesses, the key demographic for turning the tide and transforming the culture are managers. Of course, the Leadership Team has to be fully committed first, or this stands no chance.

But assuming that commitment is there, the next stepping stone is to cascade this to managers. A few will discover they don't align with the Core Values, and under the persistence of lived Core Values at play, they will likely depart. Others will adjust and get on board, and others will enthusiastically adopt them quickly.

What happens when you have both the Leadership Team and managers living out and communicating with Core Values regularly? A critical mass develops. The people most responsible for driving the company forward are now arrows pointing in the same direction. This is when intentional culture plants deep roots.

BE CREATIVE ABOUT REINFORCING CORE VALUES

One of our clients gives out the Five Buckle Boot Award to their Core Values Person of the Year. The winner has their name engraved on the side of the boots, and the year they won. Then on the bottom of the soles, all the company's Core Values are engraved on the soles.

Besides being just a fun idea, this is a terrific reinforcement of the culture. Someone is being called out and recognized for exemplifying the Core Values over the course of an entire year with something unique and special. That means the Leadership Team is demonstrating that they truly take notice and it really matters.

Also, by engraving the Core Values on something special and in a creative way, the message is "We place our Core Values everywhere. They're our DNA. This is important."

Lastly, this gives other team members something to aim for every year.

One word of warning here. Companies are often tempted to use monetary payments or awards with tangible value when a team member exhibits Core Values. This has the best of intentions, but it's a slippery slope when you introduce a get-paid-for-it mentality.

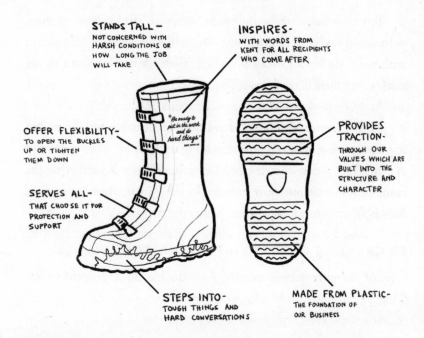

STANDS TALL — NOT CONCERNED WITH HARSH CONDITIONS OR HOW LONG THE JOB WILL TAKE

INSPIRES — WITH WORDS FROM KENT FOR ALL RECIPIENTS WHO COME AFTER

OFFER FLEXIBILITY — TO OPEN THE BUCKLES UP OR TIGHTEN THEM DOWN

Be ready to put in the work and do hard things.

PROVIDES TRACTION — THROUGH OUR VALUES WHICH ARE BUILT INTO THE STRUCTURE AND CHARACTER

SERVES ALL — THAT CHOOSE IT FOR PROTECTION AND SUPPORT

STEPS INTO — TOUGH THINGS AND HARD CONVERSATIONS

MADE FROM PLASTIC — THE FOUNDATION OF OUR BUSINESS

Core Values are about heart and soul, and when you mix in material rewards for demonstrating them, you're sending the wrong message. It's as if you're saying that the action itself isn't merit enough. Napoleon Bonaparte summed this idea up well:

"There's no amount of money that will induce a man to lay down his or her life, but they will gladly do so for a bit of yellow ribbon."

WHAT'S HOLDING SOMEONE BACK?

As you begin to institute these changes, it's natural that some people will adapt and adopt quicker than others. As the Core Values become embedded deeper and deeper into your organization, it will become more uncomfortable for those team members who aren't 100 percent bought into your Core Values, and some will depart, voluntarily or otherwise (more on this in a later chapter).

You may have others that seem to be sending mixed or neutral signals about the values. If your Spidey senses are telling you the person isn't engaged, or is having trouble adapting, you may be tempted to silently move on for now.

After all, they aren't speaking out against it or anything like that. It's just body language and a general feeling that they're not sold on this new culture. You can probably let that go, right?

No. This is something our EOS Implementers make a special point of advising businesses: Sweeping potential issues under the rug helps no one. Don't ignore People issues just because you can't quite name them yet. Find ways to bring the problems to light and deal with them.

Just start by asking questions. Here are some guidelines for bringing out what is holding someone back:

- If you suspect it's a painful underlying issue, one-on-one is the best choice for addressing the issue.
- Use open-ended questions to probe; anything that can be answered with a simple yes or no will not be helpful.
- An artful use of humor can be your friend in many of these situations.
- Don't assume that the person is just being resistant without a good reason or that they're not open to change. They may just need more reasons to trust, or there could be something they need to get off their chest first.

These guidelines for engaging and coaching can be applied widely to tackle a range of issues. Vocalizing when something doesn't feel right and asking questions are hallmarks of a culture rooted in abundance and love.

THE CONNECTION BETWEEN LOVE AND ABUNDANCE MINDSET AND CORE VALUES

There might be a question in your mind about the love and abundance mindset we discussed in chapter 2. Are we saying love and abundance is a mandatory Core Value?

The short answer is that there are no mandatory Core Values. As we have pointed out in several places, your organization's Core Values need to be uniquely you.

A good way to think about it is this: without an underlying mindset oriented toward love and abundance, all your Core Values and attempts at an intentional culture will be hollow at the center.

When you and your organization are tested with a situation where sticking to your Core Values is challenging, you'll find out then if you truly are rooted in love and abundance or if there's something deeply inauthentic at the heart of what you say you believe.

HOW DEEP IS YOUR COMMITMENT?

As we have been emphasizing, creating an intentional culture rooted in Core Values and abundance and love needs to come from a place of authenticity.

This takes sustained effort, and there will be inflection points where you'll reveal to your people what kind of leader you truly are. They will notice—trust us.

Changes happen, sometimes in reaction to outside forces and sometimes unexpectedly from within. When the heavy winds of change come, will your values reveal a solid inner core?

This question became front and center at EOS during 2021 when we transitioned to a new franchise business model. We will let Expert EOS Implementer Alex Freytag tell the story in his own words:

> In 2021, EOS Worldwide made the enormous decision to become a franchise organization. This meant that all four hundred EOS Implementers would be required to transition from essentially being subscribers to becoming franchisees. As part of this process, we each had to review and sign a lengthy franchise agreement that included lots of corporate legalese.
>
> It was a stressful time, coming on the heels of the pandemic, with lots of uncertainty. The Leadership Team of EOS Worldwide assured us this was the best path for the Greater Good of the organization. They explained why we needed to do this, and they helped the community understand how this would protect us as a community and as a brand and how we would all benefit. Kelly Knight assured us that their goal was to be the most "unfranchise" franchise model ever.
>
> Of course, we're all passionate about helping entrepreneurs, and this franchise corporate-speak was just the technical part of becoming a franchise organization. What we really needed to know was how this would play out in the real world. The Leadership Team scheduled numerous virtual town halls and open forums to educate EOS Implementers, to candidly answer all our questions, and to address all the concerns we had.
>
> The key was they were an open book. Over the next year, as the franchise agreements rolled out state by state, over 82 percent of the EOS Implementers ended up signing the agreements.

As we look back on this historic transition, it's clear that the EOS Implementers who chose to sign the franchise agreement and stay in the community held deeply shared Core Values. This move to franchise had really tested our conviction, but our Core Values were the guiding star that kept us moving forward.

We trusted the Leadership Team's decision. We knew they would do the right thing for us. We trusted in their humble confidence and their abundance mindset, and we made the leap with them. It's clear now in 2023, as we have doubled the number of Professional EOS Implementers since then, that it worked out beautifully.

Today, EOS Worldwide continues to filter every decision through our Core Values. They're the foundation that tell us what to do, whether it's about how to handle a licensee situation or where to invest profits. Although we are occasionally dinged as somewhat cultish, the truth is our community is full of trust and full of love. And because of that, there is very little fear. It's a unique and refreshing culture, and it breathes freedom for us all.

Your tests will of course be different. But there will be inflection points when sticking to your company's Core Values and practicing heart-centered leadership may feel risky, or even have the potential to impact your bottom line.

The question you may ask yourself when presented with a business challenge is this: What will you do?

REFLECTION QUESTIONS

1. Are you intentionally rewarding and recognizing your people based on your Core Values?
2. Are there any areas in your leadership that may be perceived as inauthentic while living out your Core Values?
3. Are your managers leading by example in their words and actions to perpetuate your Core Values?

• • • • • • • • • • • • • • • • • • •

"During the worst of it, we huddled around those values like a low burning fire—it was the only thing keeping us warm, the only thing keeping us alive."

When the pandemic hit, and hit fitness hard, we were left scrambling in a very uncertain time. Our revenue streams shut off overnight. We had zero visibility into when our studios would reopen; our Core Values were all we had then. During the worst of it, we huddled around those values like a low burning fire—it was the only thing keeping us warm, the only thing keeping us alive.

And then, with the values truly front and center—maybe for the very first time in our company's history—an interesting thing started happening. Some people started quitting, and some people started performing better than ever before. As we emerged from the fog of 2020 and 2021, we were surrounded by a team who truly embodied our Core Values, and we were finally ready to perform at our highest potential.

In 2022, we exceeded every single pre-pandemic peak we'd set for our company, and we were doing it with fewer people and on a tighter budget. Today, we're finally a company that truly hires, fires, reviews, and rewards around our values, and we're a better company for it.

—Tyler Quinn, Founder and CEO of Alchemy

CHAPTER 6

THE PROVEN TOOLS AND STRATEGIES TO BUILD AN INTENTIONAL CULTURE

"I AM A BIG BELIEVER IN EARLY INTERVENTION AND STRONG INTERVENTION, BUT YOU HAVE GOT TO USE THE RIGHT TOOLS. YOU HAVE GOT TO USE THE RIGHT TOOLS, AND THOSE TOOLS ARE DIFFERENT FOR DIFFERENT SITUATIONS."

— TEMPLE GRANDIN

As you retrain your culture to think and talk in the language of your Core Values, you and your team also need to have the right tools to reinforce the culture you're building.

Many business initiatives, even good ones, get tossed onto the failure pile because there was nothing in place to create consistent action and follow-up. The right tools give a business the habits and consistent behaviors that turn a vision into reality. In other words, you get Traction.

EOS tools are the steady, organized way to ensure that you and your team are following through on purposely creating an intentional culture. Your organization needs objective tools and frameworks to make correct decisions about people. Leaders who are serious about intentional culture need these tools and strategies; otherwise you're just guessing.

You may be feeling overwhelmed at this point in the book. You have a clear vision of the culture you want to create, but don't know how to get started. As the saying goes, "How do you eat an elephant? One bite at a time." The EOS Process is designed to help you eat that elephant and build the culture you want, one bite a time.

WHAT THIS CHAPTER DOES AND WHY

Many of the tools in this chapter are well explained in other EOS books (especially *Traction, How to Be a Great Boss,* and *Rocket Fuel*). Rather than repeat those books, we want to give you the basics of each of these tools in an order that's easy to follow.

Think of this chapter as the quick-and-easy reference guide to what you and your team need to do consistently to get your People Component working to maximum effectiveness. All the EOS tools will holistically help you build a great culture but there are a few that will help you produce the biggest results in the least amount of time.

We suggest putting a bookmark in this chapter and skimming through it anytime you're hitting a rough patch building your culture.

If there is a problem, the likely culprit is you're failing to implement one of these key tools. Use this chapter as your quick guide to get back on track.

Where appropriate, we will also add in explanations and comments to help with common trouble spots and potential traps that we see frequently.

THE KEY EOS TOOLS FOR BUILDING AN INTENTIONAL CULTURE

THE FIVE FOUNDATIONAL TOOLS

EOS has twenty tools in the EOS Toolbox. However, we believe in the 20 percent that will produce 80 percent of the results. In other words, what are the tools that will drive your culture forward with the least amount of effort in the shortest amount of time? The Five Foundational Tools are that 20 percent:

- The Vision/Traction Organizer (V/TO)
- The Accountability Chart
- Rocks
- Meeting Pulse
- Scorecard

If you get your Leadership Team using these tools masterfully, you'll immediately begin seeing an impact on your journey to building an intentional culture. If you get 80 percent of your entire company using these tools, you'll make a dent in your universe.

The **Vision/Traction Organizer** is the single most powerful way to document your vision and plan and get your team 100 percent on the same page with where you're going and how you'll get there. You must have a complete V/TO that your Leadership Team believes in and you use it daily to make decisions.

    Intentional Culture Connection: The V/TO is crucial for making decisions about the Greater Good. It provides objective standards and measures for what is the Greater Good. Without it, how will you judge if your intentional culture is pointed in the right direction? [See chapter 10 for more about this.]

The Accountability Chart is a living and breathing document you use to create clarity for each of your people and what is expected of them. It's meant to be constantly updated and easily accessible to everyone in the organization.

    Intentional Culture Connection: This is your first concrete step in forming an intentional culture. You have to get structure in place, or you'll constantly spin your wheels. Then once it's in place, it needs to be constantly updated to keep the business intentionally headed in the right direction. [See chapter 3 for more about this.]

Rocks are the three to seven biggest priorities in the business. Rocks help keep your company focused for ninety days. You have company, departmental, team, and individual Rocks. Everyone should be focused on at least one Rock per quarter.

Intentional Culture Connection: Building an intentional culture without Rocks would be like trying to build a house without tools and materials or a defined project schedule. Your entire team needs to be working toward the V/TO, and Rocks are the specific tasks that are tied to the 1-Year Goals. Otherwise, your team is a random assortment of human energy arrows pointed every which way.

Having a great weekly **Meeting Pulse** is the key to making sure everyone is in the know and is staying accountable to achieving results. Each week you come together and review your numbers and priorities, and get an update on your people. You review your To-Do List and solve your key issues.

Intentional Culture Connection: Haphazard cultures have haphazard meetings. Which wastes a lot of time and energy and often keeps you going in circles. The structure and consistency of Level 10 Meetings are a perfect reflection and match of an intentional culture.

A **Scorecard** helps you have a complete pulse on the businessv. A great scorecard is five to fifteen numbers that are leading indicators to how your business is doing.

> Each person on the team has at least one number they're accountable for delivering to the business each week.
>
> **Intentional Culture Connection:** Without objective accountability standards, people can stay in the wrong seats forever. Scorecards are a way to gauge if someone GWCs their seat.

ROCKS

Here's an excellent summary of the concept of Rocks from *How to Be a Great Boss*: "These are quarterly key priorities (often referred to as goals, objectives, or initiatives). We prefer to call them Rocks. It's vital that you and your direct reports agree on the one to seven most important priorities that they must complete in the next ninety days." *How to Be a Great Boss* also gives the five cooperative steps of the Rock Setting Process:

Step 1. Share your company's Vision/Traction Organizer (V/TO) with your annual Goals and quarterly priorities (Rocks) with all your people.

Step 2. Create your team's Issues List—topics that include obstacles, barriers, problems, ideas, and so on.

Step 3. With the company's Goals, Rocks, and your team's Issues List as context, ask your direct reports, "What do you see as the most important things to get done in the next ninety days?" Discuss and debate as a team and come to an agreement on the three to seven priorities for the next ninety days.

Step 4. Make them SMART (specific, measurable, attainable, realistic, and timely).

Step 5. At the end of the Rock setting process each of your direct reports should be clear on their Rocks for the quarter.

LEVEL 10 MEETINGS

Behind the name Level 10 is the reality that most people rate their meetings as mediocre at best. On a scale of one to ten, they're usually a four or five. The Level 10 Meeting does exactly what it says: bring meetings up to the highest level.

The secret to raising your meetings to a higher level is to use a proven, repeatable framework that maximizes effectiveness and efficiency.

Some good rules for effective Level 10 Meetings:

- They're scheduled for the same day and time each week, and they always start and end on time (see weekly Meeting Pulse below).
- Leadership Team meetings should be ninety minutes. Departments can vary but are usually one hour.
- Generally, three to seven attendees is the sweet spot for an effective, productive meeting.

The agenda should be the same each week:

- Sharing personal and professional bests/good news check-in
- Scorecard Review: five minutes
- Rock Review: five minutes
- Customer/Employee Headlines: five minutes
- To-Dos: five minutes
- Identify, Discuss, Solve (IDS): sixty minutes

- Note: IDS is the heart of a Level 10 meeting. The person raising the issue has the responsibility to clearly *identify* it. Then the team *discusses* it, with the objective of getting to the root cause. After a thorough examination of all the details, the team decides on the best way to *solve* the issue permanently.
- Conclude: five minutes

A quick note on the *conclude* step of the Level 10 Meeting. This is one of the most important steps of the Level 10 Meeting and the most often missed. It's vital to culture building and driving organizational clarity.

In Patrick Lencioni's book *The Four Obsessions of an Extraordinary Executive*, he discusses the importance of overcommunicating to create organizational clarity. He gives the following tips to communicating key messages:

- Repetition
- Simplicity
- Multiple Mediums
- Cascading Messages

The concluding step of your Level 10 Meeting, throughout the organization but starting with your Leadership Team is your opportunity to drive organizational clarity. You start by recapping your To-Dos and each member of the team sounding off, "Got it." Every member of the team must be clear on their marching orders for the week.

You then decide if anything was discussed or decided in the meeting that needs to be communicated to anyone outside of the team. Make sure those messages are simple and clear. We suggest you send out that message using multiple mediums (e.g., Slack message, phone call, or email a video). Someone on the team takes a To-Do to send the message.

Finally, you rate the meeting one to ten, with ten being the best. If anyone rates the meeting an eight or lower, you ask why so that the team can course correct and you get better and better each week.

WEEKLY MEETING PULSE

The Level 10 Meeting isn't just for the Leadership Team. The teams within your organization also need to commit to a regular weekly meeting. It normalizes steady communication. Without that, focus can quickly dissipate.

Committing to set times and days for weekly meetings for all your teams is a best practice—that's a good Weekly Pulse to establish.

When every person in your organization is participating in their regularly scheduled Level 10 Meetings, you'll increase productivity, communication, and team health across your entire business. You'll free up your Leadership Team to be working "on" the business versus being bogged down "in" the business issues.

A Weekly Meeting Pulse will help you create an open, honest, and transparent organization where your people are solving their own issues. Having a great meeting pulse will help you create a self-managing business that will take you to new heights and help make your vision a reality.

Every one of your meetings, especially your Leadership Team meetings, should be exciting, intense and make you tired, but most of all, they should never be boring.

PEOPLE ANALYZER

This simple, powerful tool checks for team member alignment with your culture. Here's an example:

Name	Help First	Grow or Die	Be Humbly Confident	Do the Right Thing	Do What You Say	
Herb	+/–	+	+	+	+	
Rita	+/–	+/–	–	–	+	
Curt	–	–	+	+/–	+/–	
Diane	+	+	+	+	+	

THE PEOPLE ANALYZER™

List team names down the left-hand column. Across the top, write in your Core Values. Then for each person, identify how well they live each Core Value. If they live it out most of the time, that's a plus (+) rating. If sometimes they do and sometimes they don't, that's a rating of plus/minus (+/–). And if they don't live that Core Value most of the time, that's a minus (–) rating.

The power of it is that it doesn't overcomplicate evaluations, but still provides an accurate assessment of a person's Core Values alignment. We will touch on this a bit more in a later chapter.

THE POWER OF THE PEOPLE ANALYZER

Certified EOS Implementer Randy McDougal remembers his first experience with the People Analyzer. It did not go as expected. In his words:

"I remember one of the first times I heard about EOS it had to do with the People Analyzer. One of our leaders had heard a talk and came back very excited to try it out with our Leadership Team. He explained how the People Analyzer worked, and all was going great as we analyzed each other.

"Then 'Jim' gave me a minus rating on my favorite Core Value: 'Creative.' Outwardly, I kept my game face on, but I couldn't believe it. I loved being creative. So when another leader and partner jumped in and reassured me, 'Jim just doesn't see all the creative things you do.'

"I thought those reassuring me were doing me a favor, but they weren't. It took me some time to realize Jim had given me a gift. Although I still believe I was creative in many instances, with Jim, I didn't exhibit creativity. In fact, I was always impatient for him to get to the point. I could suddenly see that my intensity and focus was undercutting me and the organization.

"I learned from that experience that every bit of feedback, no matter how I perceive it, has value. To be a great leader, you have to learn from every team member, and consider all feedback seriously."

QUARTERLY CONVERSATIONS

There is an entire chapter in *How to Be a Great Boss* dedicated to Quarterly Conversations, and it's well worth a read. We do want to add some additional thoughts based on our own experiences. Nothing we say will contradict any of the great advice from the earlier book; we want to deepen and complement what is already out there.

If you're completely new to this idea, here is a quick rundown of the basics you need to know:

- A Quarterly Conversation should happen every ninety days for every team member with their direct report. It's an informal, relational, one-on-one meeting.
- At its heart, the conversation is all about what's working and what's not working. Use the concepts of the 5-5-5 explained below to make sure you stay focused on what matters.
- Here are two great questions to help people open up: "How have you been able to use your strengths this quarter?" and "What kinds of things are preventing you from using your strengths?" You may be surprised by what these questions can reveal.
- Meetings should be on each person's calendar well in advance and be scheduled for a location outside the office.

USE THE 5-5-5 (CORE VALUES—ROLES—ROCKS) AS KEY TOUCH POINTS DURING QUARTERLY CONVERSATIONS

The 5-5-5 gets its name because companies on average have five Core Values, five roles for each seat, and a person usually agrees to somewhere between one to seven Rocks, so we'll average that out to five. The triple fives just makes it easier to remember.

The 5-5-5 helps you stay focused on what's working and not working with a team member. It creates the context for your informal Quarterly Conversations every leader and manager needs to have with each of their direct reports.

Your meetings, planned conversations, and informal communications should heavily revolve around the 5-5-5 topics. That should be no surprise since Core Values and Roles set the tone for how you do what you do, and Rocks are the specific things that need to be done. If you aren't paying enough attention to the details of the 5-5-5, you've lost focus on what matters.

WAYS TO GET THE MOST OUT OF QUARTERLY CONVERSATIONS

Any direct report should be going into a Quarterly Conversation with the mindset that it's truly a conversation, meaning a two-way street. You shouldn't go in with preconceived notions of what the person will say. If you're truly there to serve them, you need to hear how you can help them. In short, it's a great way to keep the circles connected in your organization by maintaining clear communication, collaboration, and accountability, especially between a manager and their direct report.

Remember that the point of a Quarterly Conversation is to build a great, trusted relationship that's open, honest, and vulnerable between two people.

Here are some quick tips to build trust during a conversation. We understand some of these may seem basic and obvious, but sometimes it's doing the simple things the right way that builds a great culture:

- Active listening: show genuine interest in your direct report by giving them your full attention, maintaining eye contact, nodding when appropriate, and paraphrasing or summarizing their points to demonstrate you understand.

- Empathy: Put yourself in their shoes and try to understand their feelings, emotions, and perspectives. This will help you connect with them on a deeper level and build trust.
- Ask open-ended questions: ask questions that encourage the other person to share more about their thoughts and experiences.
- Be genuine and authentic: Be yourself during the conversation. People can sense when you're not being genuine and this will damage trust.
- Maintain confidentiality: if the person shares personal information, make sure that you don't disclose it to anyone without prior consent.

Since listening is an emphasis, make it what you do *first*. Start by letting them share and show them by your actions that they have your full attention. This is one of the reasons that an off-site location is key—you don't want to be interrupted by people sticking their head in the door, the office phone ringing, and so on.

The whole mood and tenor of the meeting is also that you want the team member to know that this is a chance to be open, honest, and vulnerable. When you're digging for answers to what's not working, you don't want them feeling defensive.

Along these same lines, a Quarterly Conversation is never the place for a Strike conversation (see 3 Strike Rule below). If some kind of disciplinary action is needed, that's a separate meeting. The Quarterly Conversation should be something both parties look forward to and never be dreaded.

But that's not to say a manager should come to a meeting unprepared with no facts. Actually, the opposite. If there are things that need to be discussed and addressed, you must bring specifics, especially for team members who need more accountability to stay on track. Having examples and stories to support your thinking and observations are key to understanding.

If you say something abstract like, "I need to have confidence you'll be completing your tasks on time," that's too general. As author Brené Brown says, "Clear is kind. Unclear is unkind."

You owe clarity to each person that you manage, so instead come prepared with a statement like, "Your weekly reports were turned in more than a day late on eight out of thirteen weeks this quarter. It seems you're struggling to meet those expectations. Let's talk about solving that issue."

You're actually being *more loving* to the person in front of you when you're specific. It gives them clarity on what needs to be fixed and precision on how to improve up to the standard. To let them continue to flounder aimlessly isn't to their benefit, and not helpful to the Greater Good. A good standard is to aim to bring at least three specific examples of a behavior or issue that needs to be improved.

The same goes for the reverse. Bringing at least three specific examples of what a person is doing well is very motivating and shows that the manager is truly noticing and appreciative of good performance.

A quality Quarterly Conversation also has a feel of narrowing from the general to the nitty-gritty details. You start with the view at thirty thousand feet, very relaxed and getting the person in front of you to simply talk. As they say things, you begin bringing the picture into sharper focus with good questions—this brings things down to about ten thousand feet. Eventually, you get very specific about their Rocks and measurable goals. Think of that as bringing it down to the ten-feet view. That's an excellent conversation.

It's also important not to think of Quarterly Conversations as one-size-fits-all. There can be a tendency to think that spending more time in a conversation with one team member over another is somehow playing favorites. Or that you should be equally vulnerable with all, and vice versa.

That's a false idea of leadership rooted in a bureaucratic idea of a workplace. You're aiming for a workplace built on relational foundations. And relationships mean that different humans have different needs, capacities, and personalities. While you shouldn't give short shrift to any conversation, some folks may need a thirty-minute coffee break, and others may need a ninety-minute lunch. And the specifics of the conversation, while always revolving around "What's working" and "What's not working" can have a lot of freedom within those parameters.

DELEGATE AND ELEVATE

As we discussed in chapter 2 in the section on finding your Personal Core Focus, the Delegate and Elevate tool is one of the most powerful tools in your journey to creating an intentional culture. When anyone reaches their capacity (the number of things they need to accomplish begins to exceed the number of hours they can dedicate to work), something has to give. The wrong way—ignoring it or trying to work harder—leads to burnout, frustration, and quitting.

The solution is the Delegate and Elevate tool, and it's one of the most powerful People Component tools you can have in your company's toolbox. When you or any of your people have reached capacity, have them repeat steps 1, 2, 3, and 5 from Personal Core Focus in chapter 2.

CLARITY BREAKS

One thing great leaders who build great cultures have in common: they set aside special time to remove themselves from the grind of the everyday and step back to get a wider view of their business.

How long they go between Clarity Breaks varies, as does where they have them and how long they last. You need to find what is right for you.

Remember this isn't you selfishly taking a break. You owe it to your team to take a step back, refresh and renew your vision, and see things more clearly so you can serve others better.

Taking a Clarity Break requires no special tools or techniques. All you need is something to write with and a pad of paper. Sit down and let the thoughts flow. Here are some questions you can ask yourself to get the juices flowing:

- Am I focusing on the most important things?
- Do I have the Right People in the Right Seats to grow?
- Do I have the culture I want and is it self-perpetuating?
- Are my hiring processes designed to put our Core Values first?

MEASURABLES

Also known as metrics or key performance indicators (KPIs), measurables are the numbers that you use to determine if you're winning. Once you define your number expectations, you have a clear-cut way of seeing who is meeting expectations and who isn't.

Some business owners are already all over this, but some are hesitant to be hard and fast about numbers. It's actually showing more care and concern for your people when you give them clear expectations and they know how they're being measured. Leaving them with a vague feeling of not knowing where they stand is actually a much worse way to treat someone.

One caveat here: KPIs in companies with unhealthy cultures become competitive, and not in a good way. Measurables within a healthy culture are used to create self-correction and accountability, not cut-throat competition.

With a healthy culture, the conversation becomes, "the numbers are saying there's a problem. Why do you think this isn't working?" This is how we get people to level up, or find out they're in the wrong seat.

THE 3 STRIKE RULE

The first action you should take with anyone performing below the standard is to share with them a completed People Analyzer. Give them a chance to improve—many will. But if that doesn't work, use this (excerpted from *Traction*):

Strike One: Discuss the issues and your expectations with the person, and give him or her 30 days to correct the problem.

Strike Two: If you don't see improvement, discuss his or her performance again and give him or her another 30 days. Sometimes by Strike Two it's already apparent that the person isn't going to be able to change. It's okay in these situations to say something like, "I'm not sure this is the home for you." You may be surprised how many times the person agrees and is even relieved that someone has spoken the truth that they already know. It can be the spur they need to find somewhere else where they're a better fit.

Strike Three: If you still don't see improvement, he or she isn't going to change and must go. When the termination finally happens, all of those who are the right people will thank you for it and wonder what took you so long.

The 3 Strike Rule is essential for systematically and unemotionally removing individuals who don't share your Core Values and cannot meet expectations from your business. The best organizational cultures consist of high-performing individuals who align with your Core Values. Allowing poor performers to stay too long will have the opposite effect, causing valuable team members to leave your organization.

Is it always necessary to go through all three strikes? There can be situations where by the time you get to the second strike, you already know it isn't going to work out. This is when it can be good to tip your hand, so to speak, and say, "I don't think this is going to work out." Oftentimes, this will lead to the person acknowledging that you're right and decide to move on.

L + M = A

All of the above tools need to be seen in the context of Leadership, Management, and Accountability. Chapter 5 in *How to Be a Great Boss* is the go-to on this, but a quick brush up could be helpful.

The formula is Leadership + Management = Accountability. Some use the words *leadership* and *management* interchangeably, but they're different.

LEADERSHIP	MANAGEMENT
• Working "on" the Business	• Working "in" the Business
• Clear Direction	• Clear Expectations
• Creating the Opening	• Communication
• Thinking	• Doing

You can see that Leadership revolves around working "on" your business and thinking hard about the direction you want to go. Management is working "in" the business and is about doing and communicating. It's the two together that will create Accountability. The expectations will be clear and thought through, and they will be communicated well and followed up on.

STATE OF THE COMPANY

To build an intentional culture, your vision must be shared by everyone in the organization. To achieve this, we recommend conducting a quarterly State of the Company address where you share where you've been, where you are and where you're going as an organization. The Vision/Traction Organizer can serve as a guiding document for this address.

When you're delivering your State of the Company first ensure that your Leadership Team is 100 percent on the same page with every word of your V/TO. Make sure everyone understands the implications of executing on your vision and they understand the pragmatic strategies you'll employ to achieve it. Remember: cracks in your Leadership Team look like canyons to the rest of the organization.

A great State of the Company will create a compelling vision that your people will buy into. They will understand the implications of the vision on their personal lives and career trajectory. They will know their role in executing on the vision and be energized by it.

Be clear on what every word means and explain each bullet point if you have to. It should be communicated impactfully and memorably in twenty to forty minutes.

A word of caution: don't hold back on your vision. If you hold back on your vision because you're afraid it will scare people, you're acting out of scarcity and fear versus abundance and love. If you hold back, you'll end up with two V/TOs, the stated vision, and your secret vision. The result will be disastrous. Be bold and share your true vision with your entire company.

Please know that when you share your vision in its entirety, you'll be required to do some change management. Change is a constant in any business, and our approach to it can significantly influence our success. Jonah Berger, in his book *Catalyst*, provides a useful framework for managing change, known as REDUCE.

REDUCE stands for reactance, endowment, distance, uncertainty, and corroborating evidence. These are the five key barriers to change. By identifying and addressing these barriers, we can make change more acceptable and less daunting for our teams.

Reactance refers to the natural human resistance to being controlled or directed. To mitigate this, it's essential to involve people in the change process, providing them with a sense of autonomy and ownership.

Endowment is about the comfort we derive from the familiar. To address this, we need to emphasize the advantages of the new, while respecting the value of the old.

Distance represents the perceived gap between the current state and the proposed change. To bridge this gap, we need to make the change feel more relevant and achievable.

Uncertainty is the fear of the unknown, which can be alleviated by offering clear information and reassurances about the change.

Lastly, **Corroborating Evidence** involves providing proof that the change is effective, which can be achieved through case studies, testimonials, or pilot projects.

In the context of the State of the Company, it's crucial to communicate the vision for change clearly and effectively, using the REDUCE framework as a guide. This approach will help ensure that everyone is aligned and ready to contribute to the change, ultimately leading to a stronger, more intentional culture within the company.

Many companies, including EOS Worldwide, conclude their quarterly State of the Company address by highlighting Core Values. Employees volunteer to recognize moments when their teammates have exhibited the company's Core Values and express their gratitude (called "Core Values callouts"). This practice encourages everyone to embody the Core Values, as people appreciate being recognized and celebrated for their contributions.

These are the key tools and concepts of EOS and the People Component. Return to this chapter regularly and review all of the above. Are you and your team using all of these, and using them consistently? If not, you'll struggle mightily to install an intentional culture.

DON'T FALL INTO THIS COMMON TRAP

As you implement and make these tools a habit, there is a common stumbling block that can pull in the opposite direction of the positive tools and strategies outlined in this chapter. Understand how secrets and whispered complaints can undermine your overall efforts and then eliminate them from your culture.

BE AN ANTISECRETS ORGANIZATION

In our experience working with a wide spectrum of businesses, one of the most common instigators of people problems are secrets. Jim complains to Amanda about John's lack of accountability on the latest project, or Jane's chronic lateness, or Tom's dragging his feet on… well, you get the idea.

But they don't really want anything done about it, at least if it requires any confrontation on their part. This happens across all levels of an organization—complaining has a wonderful way of going every which way. It's called triangulation, and it's toxic to building great, trusting relationships.

EOS Implementers sometimes hear these complaints from individual team members directly to us. And we take a hard line on this. We tell the person, "If you're complaining to me, I am ready to listen. But be forewarned—I don't keep secrets." In other words, don't tell me anything you don't want me to address directly.

The reason for this is quite simple. Drama and negativity are the inevitable travel companions of secrets. Secrets, whispered complaints, and purposeless venting are right at home in a culture rooted in scarcity and fear.

If you want to eliminate this kind of complaining, you and your Leadership Team need to be the examples. Preach a culture without secrets and undercover complaining, and then practice what you preach. "If you're telling me this, we need to address it." And, "Why are you telling me this? Shouldn't you be bringing it up with this person directly involved?" Or another impactful question common in the EOS Implementer community "Are you going to tell them or am I? Because one of us is going to tell them."

Do this a few times, and the message starts getting through. And once again, what you model will cascade throughout your organization.

REFLECTION QUESTIONS

1. Are there any tools you'd like to start using, or get better at using, to enhance your journey to an intentional culture?

2. What's the average rating of your Level 10 Meetings? Are they effective? Are you solving five to fifteen issues per week? Is everyone open, honest, and vulnerable?

3. How well are you rolling out the Five Foundational Tools (V/TO, The Accountability Chart, Rocks, Meeting Pulse, and Scorecard) to every level of your organization?

4. Is every one of your leaders and managers consistently conducting Quarterly Conversations and using the 5-5-5?

5. Can each of your leaders say yes to each of the Five Leadership Practices and Five Management Practices (see Appendix)?

"But everything happens for a reason! Declining revenue forced us to take an honest look at all of our people. Did they GWC? Did they share our Core Values? From there, we were left with all the Right People in a lot of the Right Seats."

Our company culture started out as a Happy Accident. We were a small team of less than ten people who all knew each other well, so it was easy to maintain a healthy culture. Things were hectic, as they tend to be with a rapidly growing start-up, but it was easy to get ahead of any "people issues" before they became a bigger cultural problem. At that time, I was self-implementing EOS based on my experience working with CJ DuBe' at a previous business.

Naturally, our team grew as the business grew. Maintaining our start-up culture became impossible as more employees settled in and leadership had more to manage and less time to be involved in everyone's day-to-day. We hired with little strategy and got lucky with a few more Happy Accidents, but also a handful of clashing personalities. As frustrations intensified, so did growing pains. That was when we made the decision to bring in the big guns, and CJ joined as our Expert EOS Implementer.

We were still bootstrapping and reinvesting every dollar back into the business, but thankfully CJ's coaching quickly paid off. As soon as we were properly Running on EOS, we were able to pull our team out of toxicity and chaos. At this point, we had around twenty employees, few enough that our Leadership Team could keep up with everyone's goals and help reach them. We stayed focused on our Rocks and Weekly Meetings, and with each quarter, we continued to flourish.

With this newfound cohesion came another phase of rapid success. Our customer demand outgrew our size, and even though we had more of a hiring strategy than before, our urgency still made it difficult to find the right people and align them with our values. Our team grew four times in under a year, and we were onboarding faster than we ever imagined was possible. Several people were not in the right seats, Rocks were being abandoned, Issues were not getting solved, and as a result, business suffered. Six months later, we once again found ourselves in growth-induced cultural chaos.

But everything happens for a reason. Declining revenue forced us to take an honest look at all of our people. Did they GWC? Did they share our Core Values? From there, we were left with all the Right People in a lot of the Right Seats. We're in the midst of another growth period, but this time, we're intentional about each position we fill, and we use the People Analyzer to ensure we're making decisions aligned with our Core Values. There is no guarantee that we won't reencounter chaos, but we know that with an EOS-focused vision, it's a clear path back to the culture that makes us who we are.

—Caleb Gilbertson, CEO for Imprint Engine

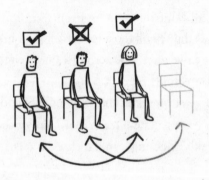

CHAPTER 7

· · · · · · · · · · · · · ·

RIGHT PEOPLE, RIGHT SEATS

"BUT I KNOW THIS MUCH:
IF WE GET THE RIGHT PEOPLE ON THE BUS,
THE RIGHT PEOPLE IN THE RIGHT SEATS,
AND THE WRONG PEOPLE OFF THE BUS,
THEN WE'LL FIGURE OUT HOW TO TAKE IT
SOMEPLACE GREAT."
—JIM COLLINS

Getting the Right People in the Right Seats is crucial for the success of your culture, something we first touched on when discussing the Accountability Chart.

Now that all the major tools for creating an intentional culture have been shared, we're in a better position to circle back and go a little deeper on this topic.

One of the most powerful things to understand about this concept is how much it simplifies "people problems." They almost all can be boiled down to one of two things: Either "Wrong Person, Right Seat" *or* "Right Person, Wrong Seat."

That's it. All the other things we get hung up on when thinking about people problems really all come down to one of those two things. That's good news. It means you can now diagnose every people problem and then see the way to solve it.

(We do acknowledge that there are situations where you need to eliminate a seat or that you'll sometimes face a Wrong Person, Wrong Seat issue. But these are more or less straightforward issues to solve, that is, you need to take action to address it quickly.)

WRONG PERSON, RIGHT SEAT

First, what do we mean by wrong person? Let's consult *Traction* for the opposite definition:

"The *right people* are the ones who share your company's Core Values."

In the same way, a person is the wrong person if they don't share and exhibit your organization's Core Values. It doesn't mean the person is creating a toxic environment (although sometimes that's the case); it just means they hold different values than your company and will cause unproductive friction.

Return to the People Analyzer for help. It will reveal their lack of alignment with your Core Values. Is the person earning a lot of minuses consistently? Is it a minus consistently in one category that's having a huge impact?

Recall that a minus means the person is violating the Core Value most of the time. It's important to keep the People Analyzer up to date (updated quarterly at a minimum), and not to focus on temporary issues or unusual Core Value slip-ups. If you're giving someone a minus, you should have at least three concrete examples (you can think of them as three data points) of where they failed to exhibit the particular Core Value.

But if a person is a consistent minus and you have concrete examples, action is needed.

NAME	Humbly confident	Grow or Die	Help First	Do the right thing	Do what you say			Get it	Want it	Capacity
Olivia	+	+	+	+	+			Y	Y	Y
Liam	–	+/–	–	–	+/–			Y	N	N
Mary	+/–	+/–	+	+/–	+			Y	N	Y
THE BAR										
RATINGS: + +/- -	NUMBER OF +: __3__		NUMBER OF +/-: __2__					Y	Y	Y

The consequences of hanging on to a wrong person for too long, even if they're in the right seat, are *toxic* to the culture. They think they can hold you hostage because of their high performance. They think, *You won't fire me. Look at my numbers.* It will drive your high performers out of the company because they know they're great, and great people want to work with great people. Also, you as a leader lose credibility when you hang on to the wrong people for too long. When you finally let these wrong people go, others often ask, "What took you so long?"

This is when you need to face up to the problem. When the person is struggling with performance or is only average, it's easier to confront the issue.

It gets a lot thornier when the person out of values alignment is also great at what they do. They nail the roles of their seat—they're truly in the right seat. But they're also wreaking havoc with those around them. It often creates a toxic environment.

Your team is surely noticing too. It's a test of your commitment to your Core Values. "Oh yeah, we believe in our values—unless you're a superstar." That's demoralizing to the entire team. What is that costing you in productivity and engagement?

We cannot emphasize this point too strongly. The Core Values must be lived and breathed by the Leadership Team first and foremost, and it must be completely authentic. If your star performer doesn't share your Core Values, they must go. No matter what.

The rest of your team will notice that you're willing to compromise the Core Values for the wrong person if they're performing well. This is a root cause of widespread cynicism. Core Values that are neither shared nor lived by the leadership are a breeding ground for employee disengagement and turnover. When you sacrifice what you say you believe for a high performer, you're doing the exact opposite of daring to build an intentional culture. You're fearfully building a culture of hypocrisy.

There are other costs too—very practical ones. You can bet people are leaving because of it. There is tremendous cost in losing someone and replacing them. It can cost up to two times the person's annual salary.

Leaders and managers rarely calculate the other true costs of a so-called high-performer who doesn't fit on values. If you calculate the time people spend complaining about the person, managing their behaviors, walking on eggshells, and doing damage control with customers and team members, those high-performers are often revealed as profit sinkholes.

You might also be surprised about what happens after you make a courageous move. We've seen the following happen many times after a problematic person leaves. Team members volunteer to fill in to take up the slack, customers sheepishly admit they "really didn't like that departed employee," and the levels of previous frustration are transformed into positive energy throughout your team.

With a Wrong Person, Right Seat situation, the only solution is to let them go. You cannot find another seat because it isn't a seat issue. It's a Core Values issue, and if they haven't reached the bar in their current slot, they won't in another.

The only solution is to summon the courage to make the call.

RIGHT PERSON, WRONG SEAT

Let's first take a wide angle view on this. The definition of someone in the right seat is:

$$\text{PERSONAL CORE FOCUS} + \text{ACCOUNTABILITY CHART} = \text{RIGHT SEAT(S)}$$

As detailed in chapter 2, Personal Core Focus are the core competencies, innate talents, or personal genius of the individual.

The Accountability Chart gives us the roles the person needs to be able to deliver on. Do they have the ability to do those roles? We should also add in GWC here. Do they Get it, Want it, and have the Capacity?

When these two fit together hand in glove, you have a person in the right seat.

When the person doesn't GWC their roles, or if their Personal Core Focus isn't a match for the seat, then we have a wrong seat problem. Let's look at one of the most common scenarios involving a Right Person, Wrong Seat.

THE LONGTIME, LOYAL TEAM MEMBER SITTING IN THE WRONG SEAT

There is a Right Person, Wrong Seat situation that business owners struggle to see, one we see often in our work with companies. It involves a longtime team member who fits all the Core Values. This person has performed well in the past—sometimes even excelled—for years, sometimes decades.

The Visionary often loves the person and is appreciative of the long service. The problem creeps in because the person is in the wrong seat. This can happen because the company has grown quite a bit, and the seat grew along with it—but the person in it did not.

Or it can be that the person's own growth means the seat is too small for them. But it no longer fits. The business owner doesn't want to look at the situation squarely because maybe there is no seat for this long-admired team member anymore. And that might be true.

But in these cases, when the issue is faced, it turns out that the team member is no longer happy. People feel it when they're in the wrong place. Everyone agreeing to ignore the problem is just another example of suck-it-up culture.

In the happiest cases, there is another seat in the company that's right for this team member. But even when that isn't true, there can be a great deal of happiness waiting for that person somewhere else. Address the problem and give them a chance to find the right seat in whatever organization where they belong.

We have later heard from clients in countless situations where after it was addressed, the feeling months down the road by all parties was, "Why did we wait so long!"

"HAVING A HEART" ISN'T AN EXCUSE FOR INACTION

With businesses we help, we sometimes get pushback against addressing this type of people problem. Their defensive reasoning is often phrased something like, "Here at ABC Company, we have a heart." It's important to recall in these situations that "putting the love in it" or "having a heart" doesn't mean letting someone waste away at work they're no longer suited for. That's not in their best interest and it isn't in the interest of the Greater Good.

The cost in real dollars of protecting someone is bad enough, but the costs in human terms are even worse. Don't let yourself off the hook with an excuse about having a heart, when the truly loving thing to do is be honest about the situation. Why hold the person hostage when they would be much happier and fulfilled elsewhere?

CREATE TIME CONSTRAINTS ON YOUR DECISION-MAKING

One of the biggest traps you can fall into is failing to set a deadline for a decision on a person you have reason to believe may be in the wrong seat.

Assuming you really aren't sure if the person is capable of the seat then select a period for them to be coached to get better. The amount of time will vary depending on the position, the business needs, and so on. If you aren't sure of a good time frame, two straight quarters of underperformance is often enough to make the call that this isn't the right person.

The reality of human nature is this: if we don't set a time limit for a decision that's going to be hard, that decision will get put off. This is more hurtful than helpful, witnessed by everyone on the team, and reinforces a less-than-optimal culture. Box yourself in by giving yourself the gift of a deadline for the Greater Good.

You're hurting your business when you fail to make a decision you know needs to be made. Keeping people around because we like them is the quickest way to become an accidental nonprofit. We have witnessed company after company make more money—often a lot more—after building an intentional culture. When you get the Right People in the Right Seats with discipline and reasonable speed, you become more profitable than ever before.

NEVER UNDERESTIMATE THE POWER OF THE ARE-YOU-HAPPY QUESTION

Sometimes we overlook the obvious when dealing with people. Someone is struggling at work, and it feels like it's going to get sticky and complicated. We worry that the person involved doesn't realize the problem, that they're going to resist change.

Try this. At some point in a one-on-one conversation or during a Quarterly Conversation, ask, "Are you happy here?"

When you ask this, if it's the right setting and done with an honest and open spirit, you may be surprised what suddenly pours out. You may get to the heart of what is bothering someone and see how you can help them fix it.

That fix might be some barrier that, once it's removed, their performance rises significantly. Or maybe it helps you find the right seat for the person in the organization, one that they get, want, and have the capacity for. Or the answer may reveal to both of you that their Personal Core Focus belongs somewhere else, and it spurs them to find their fit elsewhere.

By asking them a question with care and concern behind it, you unlocked what was holding them back. For many, it's a serious burden, because people know instinctively when they're wasting talent and not using their Personal Core Focus.

Expect to hear the unexpected sometimes, too. We had an EOS client who began focusing on having simple, open, and honest conversations about "Want It." During the course of one of these conversations, a member of the Leadership Team at the company said what would really make them happy is to operate a tattoo business.

Given that he currently worked for a highly innovative technology company, this was not the usual answer. But it was the truth, and the person was subsequently able to launch into the tattoo business, and the company was able to move on to their next level of innovation with greater focus and clarity. Open and honest conversations about happiness can be the key to realizing win-win situations.

A company called imageOne also creates win-win scenarios by doing something they call *mindful transitions*. The entire team is aware of this concept and it's even in the company handbook.

Essentially, it works like this: if someone isn't happy in their role, or if the company isn't happy with the person, a mindful transition plan is created that allows a person to have a runway to find a new role in the company or outside the company. In some cases, this has taken six months to a year to complete. imageOne works closely with the person to help them identify exactly what they want out of life and help them do the things to make that happen.

Does the are-you-happy question solve all problems of this kind? Of course not. And even when it opens somebody up to tell the truth, finding a solution to serve the Greater Good and honor the individual isn't a snap of the fingers.

But it's still a great question that will often cut to the heart of the matter, a good one to have in your toolbox.

THINGS CHANGE, SO DO THE SEATS

When we first arrive to help a business with its culture, we often find
what we refer to as Hitting the Ceiling. This happens when there is
too much work for the existing team, or the work is spread unevenly,
creating huge burdens on some. It can quickly reach the crisis stage.

What are the signs you're Hitting the Ceiling? It's a near constant feeling of being stuck, frustrated, and surrounded by chaos. No
matter what you do, you can't seem to break through.

If the crisis has been going on for a while, people are brittle and
burned out. Or even ready to close down, quit, sell: "Just, please,
whatever it takes to make the overwork stop."

It can be an emotional wringer, and most days the Leadership
Team isn't looking forward to work. Some go in every day, thinking,
I wonder if I can do one more day.

In this state, you need to start back at the beginning with the
Accountability Chart (A/C) and continue working forward to a better day and a healthier culture. Also crucial is to go back and review
the Delegate and Elevate tool explained in the previous chapter and
use it. Are you using that tool consistently, every quarter? Break-
throughs happen when people can lessen the things that sap their
energy and focus on what they're great at and what they love.

As a leader, you also need to respond to Hitting the Ceiling by
asking yourself how well you're doing at the five Leadership Abilities. Chapter 2 of *Traction* explains the leadership abilities, but here
is a good summary:

- Simplify
- Delegate
- Predict

- Systemize
- Structure

When you're Hitting the Ceiling, returning to these leadership basics is the solution.

Hitting the Ceiling isn't something you solve once and for all. As you implement EOS, growth will happen. You grow enough, eventually, you need more people. That's Hitting the Ceiling at the organizational level.

But it can happen on two other levels too.

Hitting the ceiling can happen at the department level. We have seen places where the sales and marketing department is super stressed, nothing is working, people are burned out, and the tension is thick every day. Walk a few paces down the hall, and the operations team is all smiles, and every day feels like pizza parties and confetti.

The problem again should be solved through the Accountability Chart and making sure you have the Right People in the Right Seats in the troubled department.

You can also see Hitting the Ceiling at the individual level. This could look like someone who has outgrown their seat and is bursting to grow. It could be someone who is taking up too much slack from others in the department. Or it could be that they need the budget to add someone so they can Delegate and Elevate.

You also need to be aware of personal circumstances that may mimic a problem with GWC or being in the wrong seat, but is really just a temporary situation with a life event. People have family members get sick that they need to take care of, or have a health struggle themselves, or suffer grief after an unexpected loss. Giving grace during this time and then working through the situation to get them back to full-time attention to their roles often results in the issue going away.

Of course, you'll always balance this with the Greater Good. A general guideline is that if the problem lasts more than one or two quarters, it's likely time to move them out of the seat.

Don't let Hitting the Ceiling issues continue to fester. At first, it will mean a workplace that breeds more and more resentment, and then it may lead to a mass exodus.

As the seats change and grow with your organization, it's a good reminder that a person that's a good fit for a seat today may not be the right person a year from now. This is why we strongly recommend viewing your Accountability Chart through the lens of the next six to twelve months. It's always a living and breathing document, and trying to come up with something that will work forever is never realistic.

REFLECTION QUESTIONS

1. Are 80 percent or more of your people above the bar? Do they GWC their seat and roles and share your Core Values? List any names who you think may be at risk.

2. Is there anyone in your business holding you hostage because they perform well but don't share your Core Values? Name the fear and create a plan to do what you know best serves the Greater Good.

3. Do you notice anyone on your team who is living outside their Personal Core Focus?

> 4. In what area(s) of your business are you Hitting the Ceiling? Where do you need to simplify, delegate, predict, systemize, and structure to break through?

• • • • • • • • • • • • • • • • • • • •

"As the dust settled after the termination, the cloud lifted to reveal even more significant potential and even greater revenue."

I describe myself as a balanced Libra, the oldest daughter of immigrants, a health-care provider, a mom, a wife, and a boss.

I believe in always keeping my cool, creating peace and harmony, and avoiding conflict. I'm loyal to the bones and love surrounding myself with dedicated team members who work well together and for the company. However, I dislike conflict, and I confess to sometimes being a people pleaser to a sickening degree.

You would think that a leader that so loves harmony would not stand for a toxic employee eating away at the Core Values of the company. I did a round of hiring in 2012 because my eye-care practice was thriving. I would not have guessed that one of the more experienced hires in that round would prove to be the toxic one and I would have to terminate him a decade later.

Despite the toxicity, the practice continued growing, and more employees of various ages, ethnicities, and backgrounds entered the picture, and we blended well as a work family. Until we didn't. We were having a hard time retaining new hires, had requests to shift work hours, and the work environment became narrowed down to the voice of only one person: the overconfident and highly talented toxic worker.

He was a top producer, but what is easily overlooked is the importance of company culture and how it resonates with all employees. As a company owner, it's easy to focus on things like production shifts, units sold, revenue, expenses, and the like. We were spending time on issues but with no resolutions. Why?

Because of one employee's individualism, lack of empathy, poor teamwork, and outright expression of superiority over others. It took over everything and everyone else. But who dared terminate one of their top revenue performers? What if other longtime employees resigned as a result? I did it anyway.

As the dust settled after the termination, the cloud lifted to reveal even more significant potential and even greater revenue. The quiet ones started offering opinions. Older employees voiced support, and newer staff felt more at ease. During our team meetings, the managers realized that instead of playing defense and chaperoning, they could focus on forward growth. Goals became obtainable, and everyone stepped up to cover the previous role until a new hire was made. Yes, hindsight is indeed twenty-twenty.

**—Dr. Dora Adamopoulos, optometrist at
Eye2Eye in Alexandria, Virginia**

CHAPTER 8

• • • • • • • • • • •

THE CRUCIAL
ROLE OF HIRING

"THE DEFINITION OF INSANITY IS DOING
THE SAME THING OVER AND OVER
AND EXPECTING DIFFERENT RESULTS."
—ALBERT EINSTEIN

Let's talk about pain, and let's be 100 percent real about it.

No matter how big the payoffs of building an intentional culture, there is no way around some of the growing pains to get there. Letting someone go is usually painful. Losing a key employee who didn't fit Core Values but was good at their job is painful. Living through the temporary loss of revenue after letting go of a high-performing but toxic salesperson is painful.

Businesses typically see some turnover as they drive changes to the People Component, and that's okay and often necessary. As people move to the right seats in an organization or leave because they're not aligned, openings are created. In addition, many businesses experience significant growth as their culture improves. This reveals more openings, too.

Which brings you to another fork in the road on the journey toward an intentional culture. Sometimes old sayings are right on the money: "If you always do what you've always done, you always get what you've always gotten." It certainly hits the mark when it comes to hiring and building an intentional culture.

Your new openings will be both a huge opportunity and also a huge danger.

The opportunity is that each hire that you get right adds another arrow pointing in the right direction. It's another weight added to the right side of the scale, creating the positive momentum you need.

The danger is that you'll keep doing what you've always done and end up with the same culture you already have. It's easy to slip back to Warm Body Syndrome, hiring the first person that seems qualified—or close enough. Instead of using your Core Values to check for alignment and GWC to test for suitability, you use the same standard hiring methods you used before. Old habits die hard.

If you hire like this, nothing can change long-term. You're simply putting yourself on a treadmill to run into the same old problems over and over. This will chip away at your motivation and momentum to build a great culture.

As we have noted before, we're realists. We aren't saying that you'll never make another hiring mistake. Bad choices can still slip through even with a well-functioning, intentional culture and an excellent hiring process. We sometimes tend to hire people who think very much like us and have similar experiences, instead of hiring who is best for the department or leadership role.

The more you can consciously decide to hire using the right method and criteria, the more you'll minimize hiring mistakes. Essentially, increase your batting average on good hires, and it will transform your culture.

HIRE SLOW

Let's walk through the hiring process step by step.

You've probably heard, "Fire fast and hire slow." It's excellent advice. We have already mentioned in several places the need to deal with people problems sooner rather than later, and fire fast is a good general reminder of that.

Hire slow is also the right mindset, but it needs clarification. Some people take it to mean that any hire should take months and months. But "slow" doesn't have to mean calendar time.

Hire slow is more about using a methodical process and knowing the standards you'll utilize to make decisions. It's about meeting with multiple people for the same seat instead of settling for the first acceptable candidate.

Hire slow also doesn't mean dragging your feet on a rock star. If you have a right fit candidate, move fast enough that you don't lose them. However, it's important to make sure you actually have found a rock star. Don't confuse that with the feeling in an interview of "I really *like* that person. They're similar to me and familiar. This person feels comfortable." Hiring on comfort and personality is a mistake.

The question to ask is what makes this person a rock star and the right fit objectively? That's what you need to focus on, not on comfort or your personal likes or dislikes.

Overall, the key point is that there is no reason you can't hire efficiently! Hire slow is more of a mindset than a set amount of time to fill a seat.

GREAT INTERVIEWS

You already know that interviews are crucial for finding the right hire. Reflect on whether your company's preparation matches their importance. Here are some excellent tips and strategies for getting the most out of each and every candidate interview.

Behavioral Questions

Don't make the interview a recitation of the person's resume. A quick run through the basics of their education and work background is fine, but that isn't where the gold is.

The good stuff comes out when you ask behavioral questions. A behavioral question that asks them to tell you about specific actions they've taken in particular situations. For example:

- "Tell me about a time you had your most challenging client problem and how you solved it or didn't."
- "What was the hardest sale you ever had to close and how'd you get the deal done?" And then follow up with, "And now tell me about a time you should have closed a deal, but didn't, and what you learned."
- "Share with me a time when you had conflict with somebody at work. How did you handle it and why?"

David Kolbe, CEO of Kolbe Corp, notes the importance of objective assessments in bringing different strengths to your team:

"In the behavioral interviewing process, check your bias and consider using outside, objective assessments to help you get the complete picture of how people get things done. Also, remember the importance of having a diversity of strengths on your team. Otherwise, you'll end up cloning yourself because the person you're interviewing solves problems—or says they solve problems—the same way you do. You'll naturally be drawn to that person, even if it's not what's best for the seat Assessments like Kolbe work well here."

Listen Carefully to Their Questions

We need to listen not just to candidate answers, but also to what they're asking us. This can help us determine GWC. If a person gets it, the relevance of their questions will show it. If they're fully engaged in a dialogue and are showing deep curiosity, they also likely want it. Determining if they have the capacity for it will include both how they come across in the interview and their relevant experience.

Red flag: if a candidate is asking you no questions in the interview, or their questions feel forced or trivial, that's a telltale sign that you have to find another candidate.

Caveat to this red flag: If you find this happening a lot, the problem is likely you, not the candidates. The interviewer has a responsibility to create an open and honest environment for dialogue. Many interviewers come to the end of an interview, look at their watch, close a binder, and say, "Any questions?"

Also, candidates tend to be more enthusiastic and engaged in interviews when they can sense a company with purpose and intentional culture baked in. If candidates often have few questions, the issue may be that your culture doesn't feel worth joining and your organization has no clear vision and focus.

Give the Scare 'Em Away Speech

You may have noticed that Core Values have not been mentioned yet in relation to the interview process. That's intentional. Here is a best practice for Core Values and interviews:

During the course of the conversation, you're listening hard for answers and questions that reveal a fit with your Core Values, but without sharing them with the candidate. Why not just announce your Core Values at the beginning of the interview and then ask them if they share them?

For one, how many people are going to say no at the beginning of an interview to a question like that? No one.

Two, if you share them early, they may look for ways to shade their responses to please you and match the stated company values. It's a truer test to listen for a natural fit.

However, near the end of the interview, you do want to share Core Values. A best practice for doing that is what we often refer to at EOS as the Scare 'Em Away Speech.

This is when you spell out your Core Values and give a brief example of each. You need to clearly communicate how important these values are, and that alignment with them is a nonnegotiable for getting hired and being successful in the company. Go over them one more time and then add something along the lines of the following:

"If our Core Values don't 100 percent align with yours, I guarantee we will drive you crazy, and you'll drive us crazy. It's because we truly live our Core Values day in and day out in our words, actions, behaviors and decisions. It's the basis of how we hire, fire, review, reward, and recognize each and every team member. Only those sharing Core Values will genuinely find happiness and fulfillment here, and that's why we feel strongly it's important we make that perfectly clear up front so that we both make the best decision."

You want them to really think about it and scare away those who won't work well in your culture (again, for their own good too). You're looking for those that get excited and are all in when they hear your Core Values.

You aren't only listening for how they respond to the speech but also to their demeanor and body language. Does their face light up with enthusiasm and engagement at the prospect of living in a world based on your values? Or do they cringe, cross their arms, and seemingly have a visceral reaction, making it appear they want to crawl into a hole to avoid such an environment? Or are they just meh, having neither excitement nor disdain for what you've described? Don't dismiss or ignore your gut instinct and intuition as you're taking it all in.

A follow-up question sometimes asked is, "Do these Core Values make you more, or less, interested in continuing conversations?" or for a different, even humorous approach, "Do these Core Values make you want to run for the hills?" Depending upon the role being hired, and the candidate, there are a variety of approaches to getting them to open up and be real about their feelings. Take the time to watch, listen, and be observant.

It's key to remember that a person can be very accomplished in their career, have all the right qualifications and proven experience to do what you want done, and still be the wrong puzzle piece. This would be the classic example of why wanting to hire great people is the wrong goal. That person is great for some other organization. But in your business, their approach will cause bad friction. Never hire a poor Core Values match! It will surely be an expensive decision that you have to clean up later.

NO SURPRISES

Here is a surefire way to tell if your hiring process isn't working. You end up hiring a person, and either side is surprised by what they discover after the hire. Both sides should have 100 percent alignment on values. The expectations for roles and responsibilities should have maximum clarity before any job is offered and accepted.

If you find yourself having to manage someone (outside the normal expectations), you've made a hiring mistake. If you discover a person is getting consistent minuses in the Core Values of the People Analyzer soon after hire, you've made a hiring mistake.

When these surprises happen, figure out where it went wrong and how it can help you get better for future hiring. You'll want to document what you've learned and make the appropriate changes to your recruiting and hiring processes. If you find yourself often thinking, *You're not the person I thought I hired*, examine your entire hiring process. It's likely not robust and penetrating enough.

ONBOARDING ISN'T PAPERWORK AND A FEW INTRODUCTIONS

Your onboarding process is as important as your hiring decisions, maybe more so. Companies with intentional cultures consider onboarding a continuation of the hiring process.

WHAT IDEAL ONBOARDING LOOKS LIKE

The message you send when you have a well-thought-out onboarding process is the following:

A QUICK NOTE ABOUT THE LANGUAGE OF ONBOARDING AND ORIENTATION

There is often confusion around the terms *orientation* and *onboarding*. Some companies use them interchangeably, and some use them in opposite ways. Here is how we're using the terms:

Orientation is the initial "orienting" of an employee to their new company. Things like hiring paperwork, "This is where the break room is," introductions, and so on.

Onboarding is the overall process for giving a new team member a deep understanding of your organization's culture and Core Values.

If your company uses the terms in the opposite way (orientation as the deep process and onboarding as the initial, superficial process), that's fine. As long as you're clear on the concepts and you execute well on them, that's what is important.

"We're backing up all those things we told you in the interview. We're serious about a great culture, our Core Values, and a mindset of abundance and love."

In the best of all possible worlds, you'll make onboarding a "Go Slow to Go Fast" experience. A ninety-day onboarding where the new hire is set up with a plan to fully absorb the company culture and the specifics of their roles is ideal. You're laying the foundation for tremendous future progress.

We realize not every company can necessarily afford to do that in every situation. However, at a minimum, a business needs to consider the trade-offs they're making if their onboarding feels rushed and doesn't set up new hires for maximum success.

CHECKLISTS

Every new hire should be given two checklists. One is a general checklist that goes to every new hire in the company. It's tasks to be accomplished during the onboarding time frame.

The second checklist is one that aligns with their function and roles on the Accountability Chart specific to their role.

Don't skip over this step. Checklists are a great tool from the organization's point of view because it makes sure nothing important gets overlooked during onboarding. But what you might not realize is how good this also looks and feels to the new hire.

One EOS client who is particularly concerned about maintaining a high level of professional excellence created a Professionalism 101 onboarding checklist to ensure all team members are crystal clear on expectations. This is a great example of how to think about checklists and customizing them based on your specific culture.

Checklists make the new team member realize:

- "THIS IS AN INTENTIONAL AND WELL-STRUCTURED PLACE."

- "MY TEAM/BOSS/ORGANIZATION CARE DEEPLY ABOUT HELPING ME GET THIS RIGHT."

- "I AM EMPOWERED—THIS CHECKLIST ALLOWS ME TO NAVIGATE THROUGH MY OWN ONBOARDING."

- "I AM BEING SET UP FOR SUCCESS HERE."

A WELL-THOUGHT-OUT ONBOARDING
IS "PUTTING THE LOVE IN IT"

To return for a moment to the theme from chapter 2, a great onboarding experience is a way to show Genuine Care and Concern for individuals.

All of us can remember what it's like to start a new job. It's a stressful transition in many ways, no matter how much you're looking forward to it and no matter how suited you are for the position.

A new role is going to tax your brain as you learn new systems and methods. So it's an intellectual transition.

You also meet new people all day, all week, and sometimes over the course of a month or quarter (for a ninety-day onboarding). Even if you're a natural extrovert (and, of course, not everybody is), it can be stressful and overwhelming. So it's a social transition, too.

It's also a change to your patterns. When a team member reports to a physical office, there will be a new commute and potentially different shift times. So it's also a habit transition.

During all these transitions, giving a person the anchor of a clear onboarding structure is a way to show them your culture is rooted in care and concern for team members.

ORGANIC ONBOARDING

If your culture is truly intentional and everyone is living out the Core Values, there will also be some natural onboarding that occurs, and this is super impactful. If a new team member hears about the Core Values from the Visionary, Integrator, and Leadership Team during the onboarding process that has some effect. If they hear it again from their manager, the impact increases.

But when they hear Core Values language coming from team members across the board, they truly get it. This is a company that's intentional and lives their values.

WHY ALL THIS MATTERS

It sounds a little odd the first time you hear it, but new hires are in an ongoing assessment of whether they will be staying with your company long-term in the first two weeks.

If you pause and think about this for a second, this makes great sense. How long does it really take for a person to catch onto what is going on around them? Humans are very intuitive. They may not be able to diagnose exactly what is wrong within a few weeks, but they know when they're in a chaotic culture, or something just doesn't sit right.

Of course, it works both ways; they also can lock onto the positive vibes of an intentional culture built around shared values. They think, *Here finally is a place where people are valued and I can bring my abilities to contribute with purpose.*

Don't underestimate how powerful great hiring and onboarding are for building an intentional culture.

REFLECTION QUESTIONS

1. How successful is your current hiring process in finding and assessing Right People, Right Seats?
2. Do you give adequate time and attention to your onboarding process?

3. Do you have an onboarding process that allows new hires to fully GWC their seat? Do you give them enough time or do you expect them to hit the ground running?

. . . .

"The EOS Process helped Kolbe refine a powerful set of Core Values and make them an integral part of the hiring, firing, and engagement process."

Kolbe Corp's journey began nearly fifty years ago, and over time, it has built a unique culture that centers around the understanding of conative strengths. This approach has been instrumental in developing a workplace where employees are empowered to be themselves and their diverse strengths are valued.

Yet, despite its success, Kolbe Corp recognized the need to be more intentional and systematic about its culture. This is where running on EOS proved to be key. Kolbe had a set of ground rules for a long time. However, these rules weren't always documented, and the Leadership Team wasn't always intentional about ensuring people understood them, used them in reviews, or communicated them consistently.

The EOS Process helped Kolbe refine a powerful set of Core Values and make them an integral part of the hiring, firing, and engagement process. These values have allowed the company to stay true to its mission, reorganize its Leadership Team, and attract the right people for the right roles.

The COVID-19 pandemic was challenging for everyone, but Kolbe Corp's use of EOS proved instrumental. By having the right team in the right seats, the company could maintain its focus on project work, track data clearly, and support the business's best interests.

Put differently, Kolbe was able to double down on being Kolbe because the operating system was taken care of. As Kolbe Corp continues to evolve, one thing remains constant—its commitment to understanding and valuing the conative strengths of its employees. Through its culture, Kolbe Corp has shown that reaching your mission becomes much more attainable when you create an intentional culture where people can thrive.

—David Kolbe, CEO of Kolbe Corp

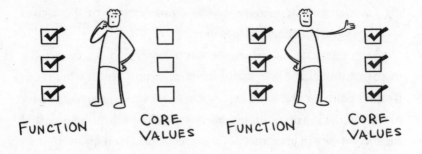

CHAPTER 9

· · · · · · · · · · · · · ·

TURNOVER, RETENTION, ATTRACTION

> "A COMPANY IS ONLY AS GOOD
> AS THE PEOPLE IT KEEPS"
> — MARY KAY ASH

By this point in the book, you probably have spotted a pattern. Show you the dream of an intentional culture—which *can* be made a reality—but also give it to you straight on what it costs.

We want to communicate how business-changing and life-changing building an intentional culture truly is, but also seasoned with a realistic portrayal of some of the pain to get there.

This chapter continues that pattern; we want to share how it feels as turnover creates change, but also how great it feels when you reach the stage where your business has a waiting list of people who would love to work for you.

Think of it as a road map to what you may encounter on the journey.

TURNOVER

No one likes turnover. Every time a person leaves your business it causes disruption and change. Sometimes that change is for the better and sometimes it isn't. Teams go through stages of development to reach peak performance. According to Bruce W. Tuckman, who researched group dynamics in the 1960s, teams go through four stages of development of Forming, Storming, Norming, and Performing.

Every time you change the team dynamics you go back to the first stage of *forming* where performance is not at its optimal state. When you don't have the Right People in the Right Seats, you may never reach the *performing* stage and so some turnover may be necessary.

"GOOD" TURNOVER

When we say "good" turnover, we don't intend to be glib about it. We understand that these are people's lives, and that change and temporary dislocation is painful. It isn't our intent to minimize that with the word *good*.

However, it should be clear by this point in the book that letting a person continue to waste away their life isn't good either. And to let someone drag down the Greater Good isn't okay either. So compared to the other options, it's "good" turnover.

Still, it can feel alarming. The experience of businesses will of course vary, but it does sometimes happen that turnover can become significant at the beginning of the process.

Even if that turnover is for all the right reasons, business owners sometimes come to us and say, "I'm getting a little scared here. Is this working? Because it feels like we're losing a lot of people."

We respond with questions of our own:

- Did the people leaving share your Core Values?
- Did they sense that the organization was determined to change and build an intentional culture and they were not on board with that?
- If it was someone from the Leadership Team that left, were they good at leading—that is, were they actually leaders?

Most of the time, the answer to these questions is no. And in that case, the turnover is addition by subtraction, meaning that more is often gained by removing team members who aren't bought into your vision, which includes Core Values.

Think of it as a classic situation of, "this is going to get worse before it gets better." It feels like treading water at best, or even losing ground, but what you're really sensing is cultural transformation.

Here's a great example of what we mean.

In 2014, Mark Crockett, owner of Crockett Facilities was introduced to the book *Traction* and decided to hire Alex Freytag as his Expert EOS Implementer. Mark is a Visionary who had been "hitting the ceiling" for several years and knew that major changes to the Crockett foundation had to be made.

After Focus Day, he was also in the Integrator seat, and within a week, after losing his operations lead, he was also running the operations team. He felt like he'd taken two steps back, but he was assured by his EOS Implementer that he and his team would soon be taking ten steps forward. Today Mark has a full Leadership Team and no longer has to fill multiple seats. He can concentrate solely on the Visionary seat. Since starting to run Crockett Facilities on EOS, the company's revenues and profits have increased substantially, all while the market and his industry have shifted considerably. That's taking some painful steps backward to make huge leaps forward.

BAD TURNOVER

Sometimes the answer to the above questions about Core Values and Leadership qualities is a yes, and yet the person still leaves. You just lost a valuable team member who did fit your values, and you need to reflect on why. You've paid a high price, so you might as well get a great lesson from it. What is happening in your organization that someone would leave when the answers to the above questions are all a yes? Don't squander such a beautiful, painful, and terrifying lesson!

PATTERNS IN TURNOVER

Are you tracking turnover if leaders and managers are leaving? If you're seeing departures centering around a particular member of the Leadership Team or departmental manager, what does that mean? Are more departments prone to departures than others? You need to investigate. Finding common threads among turnover is key to identifying and getting to the root of the issue.

One of the more likely answers is that a particular leader or manager is failing to develop those who report to them. This is a lack of leadership; developing people is a crucial part of their role. This can have a cascading impact if managers are also not being shown how to develop their own direct reports. These issues need to be proactively solved before they become weeds choking a business.

The Accountability Chart is a great tool for spotting patterns. Print out a copy of the A/C and circle all the issues. Are they pointing to a significant issue with a Leadership Team member or a particular manager?

DISENGAGEMENT IS A BIG RED FLAG

Are you keeping your radar up? Watch for situations like this:

The Leadership Team is working hard on solving an *operations* issue, and the only person not engaged is the *operations* manager. We've seen it many times. You need to be on the alert for situations like this and allow yourself to see it. Understand that the disengaged person will be part of the good turnover and make peace with it.

A person with flaws but who is engaged can often correct things when they're coached. But there is absolutely no cure if the person won't engage.

RETENTION

Surveys, polls, and all sorts of data back this up: a person's immediate supervisor has the biggest impact on whether they stay in their current position or jump ship. This is why looking for the patterns in turnover is so important.

But what else can you do to help retention? The number one thing you can do is something we will call Connect the Rocks.

CONNECT THE DOTS BY CONNECTING THE ROCKS

People need to feel purpose and meaning, especially when it comes to the work they pour out into the world. They want to connect the dots between the actions they're taking and what it's doing for a larger vision.

This too often is overlooked by managers and leaders. It's great to have clear Rocks and roles that are specifically defined. But team members can begin to feel like robots when all the communication centers around tactics and task-oriented commands.

The antidote to this is to make sure managers and leaders Connect the Rocks. Are they regularly connecting the Rocks being accomplished with helping make the V/TO a reality? When demonstrating appreciation, do they do more than say thank you? Or do they take time to connect it: "Thank you. What you do is important and keeps us on track toward the company goal of adding five new clients this quarter."

The more a leader can Connect the Rocks for their direct reports to the company purpose and vision, the more people you'll retain.

STOP SAYING PEOPLE ARE YOUR GREATEST ASSET

If we have heard it once, we have heard it a thousand times: "People are our greatest asset." It's a well-meaning statement, and no doubt the thought behind it is genuine. But it may not be conveying what you want it to. Assets are things, stuff for the balance sheet. They can often depreciate, and are often static. It implies that your relationship with your team is transactional.

Get in the habit of thinking of people as an investment. Investments tend to grow in proportion to how much thought, effort, and resources you put into them. The more you and your team focus on investing in the individual team members, the more long-term payoffs.

Ask: how are we helping people with their personal growth? With their professional growth? With stretching their capabilities? And living The EOS Life?

The more you can shift from the mindset of people as assets to a mindset of people as individuals to invest in, the more super-loyal, super-actualized traction you'll get with the people you'll retain.

ATTRACTION

For leaders, one of the most pleasant surprises of an intentional culture is when it becomes a magnet. At some point, an invisible line gets crossed and attracting high-quality applicants becomes less of a problem than sorting through someone seeking a specific role within any company, not necessarily yours. And that's a wonderful problem to have.

Part of this grows from a simple word-of-mouth calculation.

The word of mouth begins with your own team members. A person not engaged with work isn't likely to bring up the organization outside of work. It's just not near the top of the list they care about sharing. It's a paycheck, not a topic of conversation.

But if a person is doing what they love, with people they love, is compensated appropriately, and spends a great amount of time actively engaged in it, then talking about it with others is going to be top of mind. Their radar will be more naturally attuned when an acquaintance is seeking work, and it will be natural to talk about the fantastic organization they feel fortunate to work for.

Multiply this factor by the number of people who work for you, and then all the people each of them comes in contact with. Then consider that your organization may grow fast as your culture improves. This can become a powerful network on its own.

And also remember all the touchpoints with those outside your organization. Clients and customers. Vendors and other partners. Some of the best are going to want to come work for you, but even more will want to refer you. People notice and are attracted to a great culture, as this next example reveals.

A WAITING LIST OF PEOPLE WHO
WOULD LIKE TO WORK FOR YOU?

When it comes to attraction, we're reminded of a northern New Jersey business we worked with. The organization has five hundred employees, and three hundred of those are union jobs. The Visionary, who was also a trustee in the union, decided he was going to deliver his Core Values Speech at the union hall. During that talk, he laid out his entire vision and was completely transparent about what their culture was and how deep the level of commitment was to the People Component.

The transparency, the clear vision, and the Core Values were all very compelling. It's human nature—we're attracted to purpose and meaning and people who show they care. Once this was presented to the people in the union, *a lot* of them wanted to come work for this Visionary. The union members already working for the company also started to spread the word.

This Visionary and his company now were in the enviable position of having a waiting list of people who would love to come work there. That's the power of a culture of clarity and intention.

It's important to note another attractive component of an intentional culture. Prospective team members can see that there are no "spare parts" in an intentional culture. An Accountability Chart means that every seat is filled with the right person *and* each person is clear on their five roles. Everyone knows they're there for a reason. They're an active contributor, bringing their Personal Core Focus to the table.

This tells people that their voice matters, that they will be heard, and what they do is a meaningful contribution. There is nothing more attractive than that in a workplace.

You now have all the major components, concepts, and tools needed to build an intentional culture. Now the question is: How does this look when it all comes together and what kind of impact can it have on your business and your life?

REFLECTION QUESTIONS

1. Are your people your number one referral source for new employees?
2. Think about the last three people who have left your organization. What was the root cause of that turnover? What patterns have you identified?
3. What kind of culture do you think you'd need to attract RPRS people to come work for you? What changes would you need to make to create a culture that creates a line of employee prospects?

. . . .

"Distraught at the loss of the whole sales team, the two that were left doubled down on their Core Values and really focused on the culture of their organization."

Soon after beginning work with me, Landmark Roofing in Hickory, North Carolina, created their Core Values. But there was a problem. The owner confided in me that they just didn't feel right. So we did a deep dive into them and completely changed them.

However, this did not solve everything. The four-person Leadership Team at Landmark was split on the new values. Two loved them, and two hated them. Fast-forward a couple of weeks and the two members that hated them decided to leave the company and take their entire sales team with them.

They started their own roofing company, directly competing with my client. Distraught at the loss of the whole sales team, the two that were left doubled down on their Core Values and really focused on the culture of their organization. After a challenging two quarters rebuilding their sales team around their true Core Values, they ended the year with 30 percent revenue growth. The following year they continued to make Core Values and culture the priority and they more than doubled in size, growing from $3 million to $6.7 million. They're healthier than ever and expecting massive growth again this year.

—John Haney, Certified EOS Implementer

CHAPTER 10

. . . .

DO YOU REALLY WANT THIS?

"THE JOURNEY OF A THOUSAND MILES
BEGINS WITH A SINGLE STEP."
—LAO TZU

Once you finish this chapter and close the book, you're going to be at a crucial decision point.

Some will likely decide to try a handful of the tactics and strategies but fail to fully commit. This will lead to struggle and likely backsliding into the same old People problems. That's okay. It may happen that someday you hit obstacles and struggles that make you return to these concepts for a fresh look and a true commitment.

Some of you are likely still processing everything in this book, and you may eventually come around to a full commitment. That's okay, too. You want to be completely sure of your commitment, so when you do, you succeed.

But some of you are ready now. You've recognized your business in the stories and insights in this book, and know it's time for a fundamental change. You're ready *now* to dare to build an intentional culture. This chapter is for *you*.

THE FOUNDATION: KEEP YOUR EYE SQUARELY ON THE GREATER GOOD

If you recall back in chapter 2, we gave a formula for the Greater Good:

$$\text{GREATER GOOD} = \text{EVERY WORD OF THE V/TO}$$
$$\times$$
$$\text{GENUINE CARE AND CONCERN}$$

If this is going to work, you need a North Star for your culture, and that's the Greater Good. Let's look more closely at this formula.

The V/TO is *the* guide for everything you do in your business; it's what you aim at. We have some EOS clients who fail to get this at first. We check in with them after the first quarter of working with us, and it's clear they haven't looked at it since the last time we were there. Until they get that they need to review this every day, multiple times, they don't make a lot of progress.

Your Leadership Team should all have a printed copy of the V/TO they have with them or at their desk. They should have easy access to it electronically. This keeps everyone pointed in the right direction and gives you some objective measures for serving the Greater Good.

EVERY WORD OF THE V/TO?

You'll notice that the first part of the formula says, "Every Word of the V/TO." Why phrase it that way?

Because every word matters. It gives you an idea of how much effort you and your Leadership Team should put into crafting your V/TO. When you're distilling your entire vision down into two pages, you need every word to be crystal clear and understood by every team member.

A Great VT/O is an empowerment tool. In an ideal organization, the leadership team's most basic job is to communicate the V/TO, as in "This is where we're going." They communicate the what, without holding on to the how.

With the Right People in the Right Seats and with each team member working using their Personal Core Focus, all the human energy in your organization is unleashed.

You can then practice Letting Go of the Vine and let your team amaze you by finding the "how" themselves. They're free to do their best work and you're free to be a true leader. This doesn't mean that sometimes team members will not fail when they try something new. That's part of the freedom that comes with letting go, and mistakes should be seen as something to learn from.

Of course, none of this is an excuse to leave your people feeling on their own or on an island. You still need to develop your people, using the tools and principles in this book.

GENUINE CARE AND CONCERN

The second part of the formula is "Genuine Care and Concern." There are many ways to say this. You could also say, "Putting the love in it," or just plain "love." But because some people associate that with romantic or vague feelings, we use Genuine Care and Concern in the formula.

It's a phrase most people seem to intuitively grasp, and it resonates. We have given lots of examples of what Genuine Care and Concern looks like throughout the book, and we hope that has been helpful.

But ultimately, you know in your heart what Genuine Care and Concern is and whether you're authentically living it or not. Commit to it or don't, but be honest with yourself about it.

You may have noted that the formula isn't V/TO *plus* Genuine Care and Concern. It's V/TO *times* Genuine Care and Concern. This is 100 percent intentional, because having Genuine Care and Concern baked into your business creates a multiplier effect.

The people on your team are aligned on values, love their jobs, and stay with the company. There is a line of people out the door who want to work for you. Your customers experience the service that your purposeful organization delivers. It all works together. It all compounds as a multiplier.

This is why the Greater Good and this formula are so important. If you stay laser focused on it as your North Star, you'll always have the right orientation, as will your team. Yes, you'll still make plenty of mistakes. But they will be made up for many times over because your fundamental direction is toward the Greater Good.

WHERE COMMITMENT TO INTENTIONAL CULTURE LEADS

Dan Sullivan of Strategic Coach has a great explanation about what follows in the wake of true commitment. It's called The 4 C's Formula®:

Commitment. Courage. Capability. Confidence.

Here is how it fits together. If you make a true commitment to something, you have in a sense backed yourself into a corner. You're committed, and you can't wiggle out of it. You now are forced to summon the courage to follow through on that iron-clad commitment you made.

This forward motion from courage will lead to capability. You may make mistakes as you move forward with courage, but you'll learn, and the capability will happen. This in turn fills you with confidence. That's The 4 C's Formula® and how they interact.

This maps perfectly to what it's like to commit to building an intentional culture. If you make a true commitment to it, you're now promising yourself you won't be a coward when it comes to People issues. You'll enter the danger and do what is in the best interest of the Greater Good, no matter how painful it feels at first.

Courage has been a theme that has carried through this entire book, and that's because it's the only way to build an intentional culture. It's a necessary ingredient—period.

Of course, once you do it a few times, and your team also practices courage regularly, everyone's capability will rise. And confidence right along with it. It's an amazing journey.

But something else needs to be said. As the quote at the beginning of this chapter has it, your thousand-mile journey starts with making that single step (commitment). But notice the other part of the quote—a thousand-mile journey.

Once you go down this path, your journey is long—it never ends really. You get better at this, but your business grows along with you. Everyone's skills and capabilities grow. The challenges get bigger, the mountains get higher.

Therefore the courage required also grows. So in one sense, don't expect this to get easier, but do expect it to be more exciting, challenging, and ultimately rewarding.

THE EOS LIFE

Back in chapter 1, we hinted at the rewards that can happen when you build an intentional culture. Specifically, it gives you the opportunity to reach for the gift that's the EOS Life.

As a refresher, here is the summary of it:

1. **Doing What You Love** means that you spend every working minute doing only the activities you love to do and are great at doing. The actions that give you unlimited energy and excitement.
2. **With People You Love** means that everyone in your life— your coworkers, customers, vendors, friends, and family— are people you enjoy being around and who uplift you.
3. **Making a Huge Difference** means that you're having the exact impact that you want to have on the world.
4. **Being Compensated Appropriately** means making as much money as you want by providing value to others, helping them get what they want.
5. **With Time for Other Passions** means that you spend the amount of time you want on your passions, those things outside of work that you enjoy and give you energy.

Will you be able to meet these ideal definitions and score yourself a ten out of ten on all these every day if you build an intentional culture? No. But you might be surprised at how far you come and how close you get. Some days it does feel like perfection.

We have experienced it in our own lives, but even more importantly, we have seen business owners and their teams achieve this again and again. More on that in a second, but first we're going to make a bold statement:

If you don't build an intentional culture, you have zero chance of creating and living the EOS Life.

When your culture is haphazard or unhealthy, you'll always be stuck on the treadmill of frustration and chaos. Sometimes it will get a little better, and sometimes it will be a little worse, but mostly, it will feel like being stuck.

And this is really what it all comes down to. You're on a journey regardless, because you have a business. It will fail, or it will succeed wildly, or it will muddle along. But whichever of those it is, you'll be miserable and fearful if your culture doesn't work.

To return for a moment to how realistic getting an EOS Life can be, we can say emphatically *it is attainable*. It only sounds like pie in the sky to those who don't summon the courage for the journey. The stories are real and so are the results.

Since you're on a journey anyway, why not do it with joy, intention, and courage and live out the EOS Life?

WHAT WILL *YOUR* VERSION OF THE EOS LIFE LOOK LIKE?

The classic picture of an entrepreneur is someone who wants more revenue, revenue, revenue and more profits, profits, profits. Someone who would never turn down growth (and would prefer that growth be off the charts).

That's the image, but not always the reality. There are many who would be happy to maintain the same profit if things could just get easier to manage. And others would happily sacrifice massive growth in exchange for time to do things they care about outside of work.

EOS clients Mark Schmukler and Suzanne Morris of Sagefrog Marketing Group, LLC are a classic example. They used EOS tools to turn a toxic culture into an intentional one.

It set the stage for massive growth, success they could have navigated easily with their strong culture. But they're not afraid to turn away business. They intentionally hold back because huge growth is not their highest priority.

Mark explains why: "I am happy with my modest office in this beautiful historic home in Doylestown, PA; working with my business partner, and a great team that loves each other; going home at a reasonable time, not working weekends, and spending that time with my kids while they are growing up."

This demonstrates that there is more than one way to think of business growth.

Thought experiment: A business has maintained the same revenue and profits for the last three years. Have they experienced growth? The traditional answer is no. A good bean counter would say that it's a stagnant business.

But let's ask it from another angle. What if in those same three years, the Leadership Team and Visionary were able to go from fifty to fifty-five hours a week down to thirty to thirty-five hours a week, and they never missed any of their kids' sporting events, and when they went on vacation, they were truly on vacation? That's a kind of growth.

How you define growth is up to you. It doesn't have to rely solely on one or two traditional metrics. If you're pursuing a lifestyle business to live the life you want outside of work, the way you measure growth will be unique to you.

And it doesn't have to be about always trading one for the other. With the right team, you can both grow the business and have more freedom.

Here is a potentially even scarier thought, at least for many visionaries. What if where all this is leading is you moving yourself out of the day-to-day and into an owner's box, where your role is extremely limited? What if it means selling and getting out altogether?

This is why starting down this path and committing to intentional culture is both frightening and exciting. You don't know where the growth will lead. But you can always start a bigger journey, with new challenges.

The key is to think through what growth and success mean to you. And then you need to plan with that in mind.

YOUR PERSONAL V/TO

As you set off on the journey toward an intentional culture, we recommend spending some time asking yourself, *What do I* really *want*?

For some owners, it's more profits, more status, and massive growth. That's a great answer.

For others, it's a goal of mastery. How good can we get at delivering a world-class product or service? How good can I become at my craft of building a business? Also a terrific response.

Still others want more freedom. They want running the business to be easier and more productive, and they want the time to pursue enjoyment. Another superb answer.

There truly is no wrong answer. The only answer to avoid is, "I don't have any idea." That's a starting point, but not an answer.

In short, building an intentional culture is going to put you in the driver's seat. Do you know where you want to take that car?

In chapter 6, we discussed the company V/TO and its importance. Creating your own personal V/TO is also a valuable exercise for all the reasons we just stated. It can help you figure out where you want to go. We've included an exercise in the appendix to help you define your own personal V/TO.

TIME TO TAKE THE FIRST STEP ON THAT LONG JOURNEY

Are you excited about what an intentional culture could open up for you and your business, but also feeling a little uneasy?

We get it. Dealing with the People Component requires courage.

Perhaps as you think about all this, you should reflect on this quote from the Stoic philosopher Epictetus: "How long will you wait until you demand the best for yourself?"

Or put another way:

Will you dare to build an intentional culture?

. . . .

"Everything bottlenecked through Niall and me. We lived a life of Whac-A-Mole, and our culture lacked accountability and trust."

My husband and I opened the doors of our farm-to-table 350-seat behemoth in February of 2006, just in time for the greatest restaurant recession in history (until COVID). From the start, our clients loved us, yet Niall and I were buried under the weight of this massive start-up.

We're a high-end, urban-model restaurant in a tiny, conservative town in the heart of the Midwest. Typically, a restaurant of our caliber would be in a city with access to thousands of professional restaurant employees. Here in Effingham, 95 percent of the people we hire have never been *in* a restaurant like ours, let alone *worked* in one.

This steep learning curve produced intense difficulties in culture and training. Everything bottlenecked through Niall and me. We lived a life of Whac-A-Mole, and our culture lacked accountability and trust. We were shackled to the restaurant, and whenever we traveled, the experience of our clients suffered.

So when Jim Coyle, the man who would become our Expert EOS Implementer, presented at my first restaurant roundtable, I knew immediately that this was the solution.

It was not easy. Not a single person from our original Leadership Team remains. The healthier our culture became, the faster they fell away. The executive team we have now is amazing. They live and breathe our Core Values, they own their accountability, and they love their work. We just came out of our yearly planning session, and the level of trust and the hard conversations we had were beautiful. We blew our budget out of the water this year, and it could never have happened if we weren't working EOS every day.

Our follow-up with the entire team during our quarterly State of the Company was incredible. We started with Core Value shout-outs and cheers across the room. We then dove into areas where our values were suffering and discussed how we as a team were going to ensure that no cancers took hold. My favorite thing to say at Firefly, other than complimenting team members, is, "Did you get it on the issues list?" Having access to an issues list empowers our people, they feel heard, seen, and accountable. Our issues lists are the engines that drive our evolution. They make Firefly Grill and the lives of our clients and people better with every issue we solve.

Our family can now travel, our daughter gets time with both of us, our work is respected, and though we still occasionally feel a pang of guilt when we aren't there, that diminishes as more and more of our team members take ownership of their work. Our turnover has gone from an average of two years to an average of 4.6 years, and that includes seasonal summer help, unheard of in the restaurant industry.

Niall and I have been at this for a while. We fully subscribe to paying it forward and now have the honor of mentoring quite a few burgeoning entrepreneurs. I always tell them that in business, inevitably at some point or points in our case, in desperation, you'll go looking for a silver bullet. It will cost you pain, frustration, time, and money because silver bullets don't exist. Then I follow with this simple truth: EOS is the exception that proves the rule.

EOS takes years to master but ask anyone who has done it and done it well. They will tell you it's worth the effort. It changed everything at Firefly Grill and opened our personal lives, and the lives of our employees to a newfound freedom, joy, and deep sense of purpose.

—Kristie Campbell, CEO and Cofounder of Firefly Grill

APPENDIX

BOOK BONUS CONTENT

For book bonus content, including a free Culture Checkup tool, a Core Values Speech captured on video, and more, please visit: **eosworldwide.com/people-book.**

THE PERSONAL V/TO

The Personal V/TO is an important tool to help everyone live their ideal lives. To complete a Personal V/TO take an extended Clarity Break to answer nine questions. You can access a copy of the Personal V/TO at eosworldwide.com.

PERSONAL CORE VALUES

What are your personal Core Values? We recommend using the Values Exercise by think2perform (think2perform.com/values/). Next follow the steps from chapter 2 to create your Personal Core Focus.

10-YEAR TARGET

What is your 10-Year Target? We recommend getting in the habit of thinking in ten-year increments. As Bill Gates said, "Most people overestimate what they can do in one year and underestimate what they can do in ten years." When you write your 10-Year Target it should be written in simple language that inspires and motivates you. For example, it could be "$2 million in net worth" or "help one million people live their ideal lives."

LIFETIME WISH LIST

What is your Lifetime Wish List? During your Clarity Break, follow this process to create your Lifetime Wish List.

Step 1: Reflect on Your Aspirations
Start with a moment of introspection. Think about what you truly want in life, not just in terms of materialistic things, but also experiences, achievements, and personal growth.

Step 2: Categorize Your Wishes
Break down your lifetime wishes into categories. These might

include personal growth, family, career, travel, health, financial, and others. This will help make your list more organized and comprehensive.

Step 3: Make It Specific

For each wish, be as specific as possible. For example, instead of saying, "Travel more," specify the places you want to visit or experiences you want to have.

Step 4: Prioritize Your Wishes

Once you have your list, take some time to prioritize your wishes. This doesn't necessarily mean you need to accomplish them in this order, but it can help you focus on what's most important to you.

Step 5: Set a Timeline

Even though these are lifetime wishes, it can be helpful to have an estimated timeline or age by which you'd like to accomplish each. This can make your wishes seem more real and achievable.

Step 6: Review and Update Regularly

Your wishes may change over time, and that's okay. Make sure to review and update your Lifetime Wish List regularly to ensure it still aligns with your life goals.

Remember: the Lifetime Wish List is meant to inspire and motivate you. There's no right or wrong here—just make sure your wishes are true to what you really want from life.

CORE HABITS

Our habits create our future. Thinking about your Personal Core Focus and your 10-Year Target, what habits do you need to have in order to remain inside of your Personal Core Focus and achieve your 10-Year Target? For example, it could be that you need to have the energy to accomplish your goals so you have a Core Habit of working out three times a week. Or you need the mental capacity and focus, so you have a daily meditation or prayer habit.

If you want to go deeper and get additional ideas, you can visit the10disciplines.com where Gino Wickman shares his habits.

3-YEAR PICTURE

Break down your 10-Year Target and Lifetime Wish List into what you want within the next three years. Pick a date three years from now. What will your income be? Net worth? What are some measurables that will let you know you're on track? Finally, paint a vivid picture of what your world looks like three years from now. For example, you might add "One hundred hours serving at a soup kitchen" or "Giving talks to industry groups." This list is usually five to fifteen items you want to be true three years from now.

1-YEAR PLAN

Now that you have your personal vision created and you're inspired and motivated, break it down into what needs to be accomplished in this year. We recommend setting the date to "12/31/XX." There's no ideal time to do your annual planning and updating your V/TO, but we recommend doing this in the last week of the year.

Set your income, net worth, and measurables. Then create three to seven SMART (specific, measurable, attainable, relevant, and timebound) goals that you want to accomplish in the year that will set you up to achieve everything in your 3-Year Picture.

ROCKS

Break down your 1-Year Plan into a 90-Day World by setting three to seven Rocks for the quarter. Make them SMART (specific, measurable, attainable, relevant, and timebound).

ISSUES LIST

Everything that you know you need to deal with but don't need to worry about within the next ninety days goes on your Issues List. It could be things like buying a new car because your car is getting worn out, but it's not urgent and can wait. It could be updating your estate documents or your insurance. Anything that comes to mind that you may need to deal with but it can wait for more than ninety days.

REGULAR REVIEWS

The worst thing that can happen is you create a Personal V/TO and don't use it to plan your life. As the saying goes, vision without traction is hallucination. In order to ensure that you're gaining constant Traction on your Personal V/TO we recommend the following steps:

ANNUAL REVIEW

Every year update and thoroughly review your entire Personal V/TO. We all change over time and your goals and priorities may change. Make this a yearly ritual that you do without fail.

QUARTERLY REVIEW

Every quarter update your Rocks by looking at your 1-Year Plan and your 3-Year Picture. We all get off track every ninety days, and this review helps us course correct along the way.

WEEKLY REVIEWS

Review your Personal V/TO every week. Set a date on the calendar every week that you'll review your Personal V/TO and plan out the week to make progress on your Rocks. Update your goals and Issues List as necessary. We recommend using Time Blocking by blocking out focus time on your calendar where you'll work on both your company and personal rocks.

DAILY REVIEWS

Every night before you go to bed, review your Rocks and plan out the next day. Update, tweak, hone, and refine your schedule.

EOS
ENTREPRENEURIAL
OPERATING SYSTEM™

THE PERSONAL V/TO™

NAME: _____

VISION

CORE VALUES	1. 2. 3. 4. 5.
PERSONAL CORE FOCUS™	Purpose: Niche:
10-YEAR TARGET™	
LIFETIME WISH LIST	· · · · · · · · · ·
BEST HABITS	

3-YEAR PICTURE™

Future Date:

Income:

Net Worth:

Measurables:

What does it look like?

· · · · · · · · · · · · · · · · · ·

THE PERSONAL V/TO™

NAME: _____

T R A C T I O N

1-YEAR PLAN	ROCKS (the next 90 days)	ISSUES LIST

1-YEAR PLAN

Future Date:
Income:
Net Worth:
Measurables:

Goals for the Year:

1. _____
2. _____
3. _____
4. _____
5. _____
6. _____
7. _____

With your cursor in the last row, press Tab to add another row.

ROCKS (the next 90 days)

Future Date:
Income:
Net Worth:
Measurables:

Rocks for the Quarter:

1. _____
2. _____
3. _____
4. _____
5. _____
6. _____
7. _____

With your cursor in the last row, press Tab to add another row.

ISSUES LIST

Ideas, problems, concerns, obstacles, and barriers

1. _____
2. _____
3. _____
4. _____
5. _____
6. _____
7. _____
8. _____
9. _____
10. _____
11. _____
12. _____
13. _____

With your cursor in the last row, press Tab to add another row.

Prioritize
- Identify
- Discuss
- Solve

PEOPLE ANALYZER™

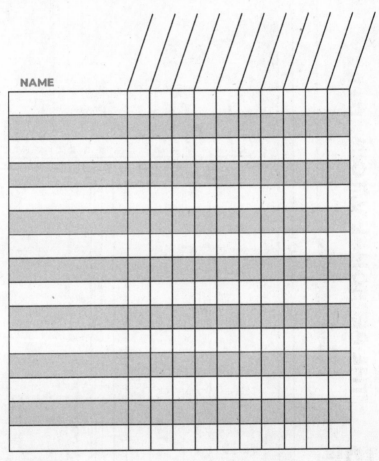

NAME

THE BAR

| RATING: + +/- - | NUMBER OF + : _____ | NUMBER OF +/- : _____ |

VISION/TRACTION ORGANIZER™

ORGANIZATION NAME: _____

VISION

EOS MODEL®

		3-YEAR PICTURE™
CORE VALUES	1. 2. 3. 4. 5.	Future Date: Revenue: Profit: Measurables: What Does It Look Like? . . . .
CORE FOCUS™	Purpose/Cause/Passion: Our Niche:	
10-YEAR TARGET™		

MARKETING STRATEGY	Target Market/"The List":
	
	Three Uniques™: 1.
	                         2.
	                         3.
	
	Proven Process:
	
	Guarantee:	

VISION/TRACTION ORGANIZER™

EOS MODEL®

ORGANIZATION NAME: _____

— TRACTION —

1-YEAR PLAN	ROCKS	ISSUES LIST
Future date:	Future date:	1. _____
Revenue:	Revenue:	2. _____
Profit:	Profit:	3. _____
Measurables:	Measurables:	4. _____
Goals for the Year	**Rocks for the Quarter** Who	5. _____
1. _____	1. _____	6. _____
2. _____	2. _____	7. _____
3. _____	3. _____	8. _____
4. _____	4. _____	9. _____
5. _____	5. _____	10. _____
6. _____	6. _____	**Prioritize**
7. _____	7. _____	• Identify
		• Discuss
		• Solve

ACCOUNTABILITY CHART™

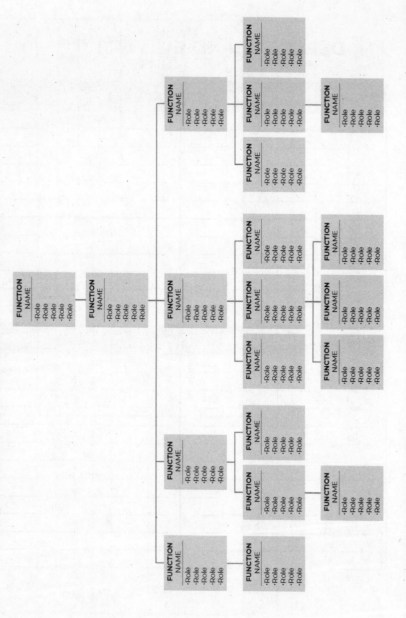

DELEGATE AND ELEVATE™

LOVE / GREAT	LIKE / GOOD

DON'T LIKE / GOOD	DON'T LIKE / NOT GOOD

▌LEVEL 10 MEETING™

THE WEEKLY AGENDA

Day: _____   Time: _____

AGENDA

Segue	5	Minutes
Scorecard	5	Minutes
Rock Review	5	Minutes
Customer/Employee Headlines	5	Minutes
To-Do List	5	Minutes
IDS	60	Minutes

Conclude
  Recap To-Do List
  Cascading messages
  Rating (1-10)
	5	Minutes

COMPANY SCORECARD

WHO	MEASURABLES	GOAL	5-Jan	12-Jan	19-Jan	26-Jan	2-Feb	9-Feb	16-Feb	23-Feb	1-Mar	8-Mar	15-Mar	22-Mar	29-Mar

▌ GWC™

ARE EACH OF YOUR PEOPLE IN THE RIGHT SEAT?

If they are not, you will be frustrated, they will be frustrated, and, as a result, you will never be able to completely delegate and elevate. You will always be forced to do their work and will not be able to let go of the vine.

In order for someone to be in the right seat, to step up, and to ultimately fill the opening you have created, they must get it, want it, and have the capacity to do the job. If any one of the three is a "no," it is never going to happen . . . 99.9 percent of the time.

FUNCTION
NAME
- _____
- _____
- _____
- _____
- _____

<u>DO THEY:</u>   Y   N

GET IT?   ☐   ☐

- Do all of the neurons in their brain connect when you explain and they do the job?
- Do they get all of the ins and outs of the position?
- Not everyone gets it, and it's not a bad thing. They just need to be in a different seat.

WANT IT?   ☐   ☐

- Do they genuinely want to do the job?
- Do they get up every morning wanting to do it?
- You can't pay, motivate, force, or beg them to want it. They have to want it on their own.
- Sometimes people get it and have the capacity, but just don't want it anymore.

CAPACITY?   ☐   ☐

- Do they have the mental, physical, spiritual, time, knowledge and emotional capacity to do the job?
- Sometimes this one is negotiable. While not getting it or wanting it are deal-killers, a problem of capacity can be solved, although rarely. If you believe the person can gain the capacity and you are willing to invest the time, resources, and energy for him or her to do so, do it. It is just that most growing organizations don't have the luxury of waiting one to three years for someone to gain the capacity and need the seat filled completely now.

CLARITY BREAK™

One discipline that all great leaders practice is taking time on a regular basis to rise above the everyday demands of their jobs to reflect and think at the thirty-thousand-foot level.

To stay sharp, confident, and at your best for your people, you must take Clarity Breaks. By definition, a Clarity Break is time you schedule **away from the office**, out of the daily grind of running the department, to think and to work on your business, department, or self.

Stepping back to think will create clarity for you and restore your confidence. This is important because the normal course of day-to-day business pulls you deeper and deeper into the minutiae of your work. As a result, you sometimes can't see the forest for the trees. You start to feel overwhelmed and you become short with your people.

MAKE THE TIME TO SAVE TIME.

Therefore, at intervals, you must elevate yourself above the day-to-day activities "in" the business so you can work "on" the business. Schedule an appointment with yourself. Put it down on your calendar. If you don't schedule the time, it will never magically happen. At first you may be concerned about when you'll find the time. The irony is, you'll actually save time by taking Clarity Breaks. When you are clear about your bigger objectives, you gain the confidence to simplify procedures and create efficiencies.

MINIMIZE DISTRACTIONS AND ALLOW YOURSELF TO JUST THINK.

Use this scheduled break wisely, though. This is not time to catch up on email or complete a to-do list. It's time to think, to see things clearly and restore your confidence. Faced with a blank legal pad or journal, with no agenda, no interruptions or distractions, you'll be challenged at first to actually think. Use these Clarity Break questions get started.

CLARITY BREAK QUESTIONS
- Is the Vision and Plan for the business/department on track?
- What is the number one goal?
- Am I focusing on the most important things?
- Do I have the Right People in the Right Seats to grow?
- What is the one "people move" that I must make this quarter?
- How strong is my bench?
- If I lose a key player, do I have someone ready to fill the seat?
- Are my processes working well?
- What seems overly complicated that must be simplified?
- Do I understand what my direct reports truly love to do and are great at doing?
- Am I leveraging their strengths?
- What can I delegate to others in order to use my time more effectively?
- What can we do to be more proactive versus being reactive?
- What can I do to improve communication?
- What's my top priority this week? This month?

▌5 LEADERSHIP PRACTICES

WHEN LEADING MY DIRECT REPORTS:

        Y N

I AM GIVING CLEAR DIRECTION ☐ ☐

- Creating the opening
- A compelling vision
- V/TO™

I AM PROVIDING THE NECESSARY TOOLS ☐ ☐

- Resources
- Training
- Technology
- People
- Time and attention

I AM LETTING GO OF THE VINE ☐ ☐

- Delegate and Elevate™
- GWC™

I ACT WITH THE GREATER GOOD IN MIND ☐ ☐

- Company vision (V/TO™)
- My actions
- My decisions
- Walk the talk
- Company needs first

I AM TAKING CLARITY BREAKS™ ☐ ☐

- "On" the business
- Creating clarity
- Protecting my confidence
- Daily, weekly, or monthly
- Blank legal pad

▌5 MANAGEMENT PRACTICES

WHEN MANAGING MY DIRECT REPORTS:

                                           Y   N

I KEEP EXPECTATIONS CLEAR   ☐ ☐

- Mine and theirs
- Roles, Core Values, Rocks, and measurables

I AM COMMUNICATING WELL   ☐ ☐

- Me and them
- You know what is on each other's mind (no assumptions)
- 2 emotions
- Question-to-statement ratio

I HAVE THE RIGHT MEETING PULSE™   ☐ ☐

- Even exchange of dialogue
- Reporting measurables
- Keeping the circles connected

I AM HAVING QUARTERLY CONVERSATIONS™   ☐ ☐

- The 5-5-5™
- The People Analyzer™ (Core Values and GWC™)

I AM REWARDING AND RECOGNIZING   ☐ ☐

- Give positive and negative feedback quickly (24 hours)
- Criticize in private, praise in public
- Be their boss, not their buddy
- The Three-Strike Rule

▌ISSUES SOLVING TRACK™

Issues are problems, challenges, or obstacles, opportunities, and new ideas worth your attention.
It's really anything—good or bad—that your team may need to resolve. With your **Issues List**
complete and clear, start by prioritizing the one, two, and three most important Issues to tackle
today. Then, follow this three-step **Issues Solving Track**™.

STEP 1: IDENTIFY

The stated problem is rarely the *real issue*.

- You have to dig down to find the *real issue*.
- Don't move forward until you clearly identify the *real issue*.
- Once you have identified the real issue, then move to discuss and stay laser
  focused on the real issue until it is solved (no tangents).

STEP 2: DISCUSS

Being completely "open and honest," every member of the team shares his or her thoughts, ideas,
concerns, and solutions regarding the *real issue*.

- Discuss and debate.
- Get it all on the table, but say it only once. Saying it more than once is politicking.
- When it's all on the table and things are getting redundant, it's time to solve.
- When the *real issue* is clear and you keep the greater good in mind, the solution is always
  simple. That doesn't mean easy, and sometimes it's very hard.

STEP 3: SOLVE

"Solve" means agreeing on a plan that will make the Issue go away forever. It's more important
that you decide than *what* you decide... so decide!

- The solution must be stated by someone until you hear the sweet sound of agreement.
- Sometimes you will have to go back to the discussion step after the solution is stated
  because you haven't truly solved it.
- Once everyone agrees, or at least can live with the decision, the action step(s) must be
  clear, owned by someone, and put on the To-Do List (where they're confirmed as "To-Done"
  at next week's meeting).

On a healthy team, everyone will agree with the solution eight out of ten times. When they don't,
the Integrator needs to make the final decision. Consensus management *does not work* and will
put you out of business faster than anything. Not everyone will be pleased in these situations,
but as long as they have been heard and the team is healthy, they can "disagree and commit" to
support the decision. From there, there must be a united front moving forward.

5-5-5™

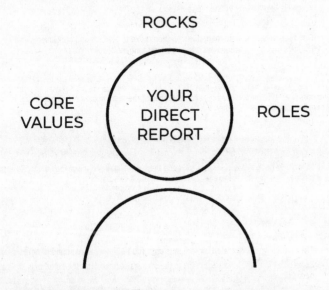

FIVE LEADERSHIP ABILITIES™

Hitting the ceiling is when you, your department, or your company stop growing. It's the feeling of being stuck, overwhelmed, and frustrated – and it's inevitable. All entities that grow experience growing pains – it's scientific. **Breaking through** the ceiling is also scientific. Your ability to break through the ceiling is in direct proportion to your ability to master these **Five Leadership Abilities**:

Your ability to **Simplify**:
- As an entity grows, so does the amount of information, details, and lines of communication. It gets more complex and chaotic, fast.
- Great leaders keep things simple – constantly looking for ways to eliminate complexity.
- Simplify the messages, processes, structure, vision, and communication.
- Ask yourself, "Is it as simple as possible?"

Your ability to **Delegate and Elevate**:
- True growth only happens when you delegate and elevate to your true skill set.
- You only have 100% of your working time. If it takes 120% to do the job well, you must delegate and elevate the extra 20%.
- The people you delegate to must be the right people in the right seats. They must share your Core Values and GWC™ (Get it, Want it, and have the Capacity to do the job well). If they don't, you can't delegate and elevate, and you must solve the people issue first.
- "Let go of the vine."

Your ability to **Predict**:
- You must master both long-term and short-term predicting:
  - **Long-term predicting** is your ability to predict and plan 90 days and beyond (climb the tree/ work "on" the business).
  - **Short-term predicting** is your ability to solve all issues on a daily and weekly basis for the greater good of the company (IDS).
- Otherwise, your organization won't have direction and the ability to prioritize. Issues will pile up and go unresolved, and things will ultimately implode.

Your ability to **Systemize**:
- Systemize means documenting, simplifying, and getting everyone following your handful of Core Processes – the things that make up your "way" of doing business.
- Take a "20/80" approach - document the 20% that gets you 80% of the results using the Three Step Process Documenter™.
- Simplify each process by removing redundant or unnecessary steps and incorporating checklists.
- "Followed By All" means you train and manage everyone to follow the process – no exceptions.
- As a result, you will create consistency in your organization. With consistency comes simplicity in management, efficiency, better results, predictability, more enjoyment, and more profitability.
- You have to systemize the predictable so that you can humanize the exceptional.

Your ability to **Structure:**
- You must take a big step back, rise above the organization, and see the big picture. As Kurt Gödel said, "You cannot be part of a system, and at the same time understand that system."
- Once you have taken a step back, you must decide what is the right and best way to structure the organization to get to the next level. Forget about people, personalities, and egos.
- Use the Accountability Chart™ to determine the right structure for your organization. It will help you identify all available seats and determine who is accountable for what.
- Get the right people in the right seats.

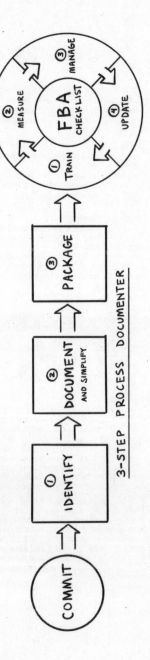

ACKNOWLEDGMENTS

MOD

- Mark P. O'Donnell
- Tommy O'Donnell
- Jill Young

CJ

- Gino Wickman
- Don Tinney
- Mike Paton
- Jill Cook

KELLY

- To key mentors, coaches and navigators on my journey: Gino Wickman, Don Tinney, Mike Paton, Mark Ciucci, Patrick Bommarito, Chris Sarris
- My special co-authors, Mark O'Donnell and CJ DuBe'
- My amazing assistant, Melissa Hellebuyck
- Dear family and friends: Aileen Ryan, Deirdre Wickenheiser, Dave Ryan, Ginny McCarthy, Nancy Distelrath

INFLUENTIAL IN OUR JOURNEYS:

- David Kolbe and Amy Bruske, Kolbe
- Dan Sullivan, Strategic Coach & Shannon Waller Strategic Coach
- Lewis Schiff, Birthing of Giants
- Gino Wickman, Don Tinney, Mike Paton navigation and mentorship
- Longstanding members of our EOS Worldwide team: Amber Baird, Lisa Hofmann, Tyler Smith
- Jill Young, Coaching team and our entire community of EOS Implementers
- Our partners at The Firefly Group, David Mann and Mark Sneider

CLIENTS AND CONTRIBUTORS

Tiffany Ablola, Dora Adamopoulos, Amber Baird, Beth Berman, Brandon Blell, Evan Blumenthal, Nick Bradfield, Gavin Brauer, Vincent Bryant, Victoria Cabot, Kristie Campbell, Chris Carmouche, Anese Cavanaugh, Debra Chantry-Taylor, Justin Cox, Jim Coyle, Zachary Cramer, Mark Crockett, Rob Drynan, Rob Dube, Jamie Duininck (with Prinsco), Beth Fahey, Kyle Fowles, Alex Freytag, Caleb Gilbertson (with Imprint Engine), Michael Halperin, John Haney, Donna Hanson, Michael Hazley, Hark Herold, Josh Holtzman, Nancy Inman, Neil James, Monica Justice, Adam Kaplan, Steve King, Scott Kuehl, Josh Kwasny, Rachel Lebowitz, Don Maranca, Julie Markee, Justin Maust, Randy McDougal, Gene Moorhead, Suzanne Morris, Rodney Mueller, Rick Nelson, Hank O'Donnell, Joe Paulsen, Justin Phillips, Richard Price, Tyler Quinn,

Sean Rosensteel, Tiffany Sauder, Gregg Saunders, Mark Schmukler, Anne Schoolcraft, Theresa Steele, Bill Stratton, Joel Swanson, Jeanet Wade, Tim Watson, Ali Wendt, Brian White, Dale Williams, Glenn Yeffeth, Mitchell York

ABOUT THE AUTHORS

Mark O'Donnell is a highly successful entrepreneur, CEO, and Expert EOS Implementer. He is the current Visionary and CEO of EOS Worldwide and has also served as Head Coach for the company. With over 100 companies under his belt, Mark has helped numerous companies achieve their goals and get what they want from their businesses.

As a serial entrepreneur, Mark has founded and sold multiple successful businesses. His passion for helping people live their ideal lives led him to his current mission of assisting 1,000,000 people with tools like those found in the Entrepreneurial Operating System (EOS).

Mark is a lifelong learner and an alumnus of Albright College, Northeastern University, and The Wharton School at the University of Pennsylvania. He lives outside Philadelphia, PA, with his wife, mother-in-law, three children, and his one-hundred-pound dog, Blue.

Kelly Knight has served as EOS Worldwide's Integrator since 2016. She's worked with eleven Visionaries to date in her career and credits her father for being the first person to show her how to take an idea and make it real.

Prior to joining EOS, Kelly honed her skills as an expert team-builder for over twenty years while leading dynamic organizations in the financial services industry. Hard-wired to find talented people and guide them to reaching their full potential, Kelly harmonizes the major functions of EOS while driving accountability and organizational clarity. Her gift is leading with positivity and heart, with a passion for uniting teams to achieve the extraordinary.

Today, Kelly's focus is sharing EOS with the world and growing the EOS community with people who are passionate about helping entrepreneurs get everything they want from their businesses and live their ideal lives.

Kelly is a proud alumnus of the University of Michigan and lives with her family in the small town of Clarkston, Michigan.

CJ DuBe' has always been an entrepreneur. With more than twenty-five years of experience, CJ knows a lot about business and people. Not following a traditional path, CJ has worked in a variety of capacities, from managing a sales team for a large international company to Director of Operations & HR for a facilities management firm. In 2006, along with two other talented entrepreneurs, CJ launched a Human Resources consulting firm. After selling it, CJ went looking for her next entrepreneurial venture and was introduced to Gino Wickman's book *Traction*. Seeing the benefits of companies implementing the Entrepreneurial Operating System (EOS), CJ had found her next obsession.

Since 2010, helping entrepreneurs and their Leadership Teams has become CJ's passion. She has helped over 130 companies, through more than 1,700 sessions, clarify, simplify, and achieve their vision. An award-winning entrepreneur with a dynamic background, CJ is also a sought-after speaker—spreading the word of EOS and helping companies and Leadership Teams get better at three things: VISION, TRACTION, and HEALTHY.

Now an Expert EOS Implementer, CJ has spent the last twelve years working with and helping to grow the EOS Worldwide community. She was a member of the Leadership Team for six years and served as the Global Community Leader for EOS Worldwide. CJ continues to serve as a Community Leader, teaching Boot Camp and facilitating Quarterly Collaborative Exchanges for all EOS Implementers.

CJ is a Minnesota native who splits her time between the Twin Cities and Arizona. A mother of seven and a grandmother of twelve, CJ is family oriented and lives life full circle.

GET A GRIP

AN ENTREPRENEURIAL FABLE: YOUR JOURNEY TO GET REAL, GET SIMPLE, AND GET RESULTS

BY GINO WICKMAN AND MIKE PATON

Learn More at
EOSWORLDWIDE.COM/GET-A-GRIP-BOOK